PARADISE REGAINED

THE TRADITION AND THE POEM

PARADISE REGAINED

THE TRADITION AND THE POEM

BY

ELIZABETH MARIE POPE

New York

RUSSELL & RUSSELL

1962

ACKNOWLEDGMENTS

For help in completing this study, I am first and most deeply indebted to Professor Don Cameron Allen of Johns Hopkins University, who directed the work as a doctoral dissertation, followed its progress since, and has given me of his time and scholarship with unfailing courtesy, patience, and generosity. I have also been greatly assisted by the custodians of the Christian Index, Dumbarton Oaks, Washington, D. C.; the Rare Book Room of the Library of Congress; the Baltimore Museum of Art; the Huntington Library; the Brown University Library; the Library of the Union Theological Seminary in New York; the Peabody Library and the Diocesan Library in Baltimore; the Goshen Library and Historical Society, Goshen, N. Y.; and the Johns Hopkins University Library. For long-suffering friendship and many helpful suggestions, I am especially grateful to Professor Raymond Dexter Havens, Frances Colby, Roy Harvey Pearce, and Mrs. Charles W. Paget.

To
D. C. A.

CONTENTS

INTRODUCTION

The immediate source of *Paradise Regained* is obviously the account of the temptation of Christ given by the Evangelists. But by the seventeenth century an immense mass of doctrine, interpretation, and legend had gradually accumulated about that narrative, and given rise to a traditional or conventional conception of the event familiar to every intelligent and instructed Christian. If he was of a conscientious or a scholarly mind, he read not only his Gospels, but the great commentaries on those Gospels composed by the Fathers of the Church and the theologians of the Renaissance, who had gone painfully over the text verse by verse and almost letter by letter, alert for every possible shade of meaning, explaining the significance of each speech or action in the light of orthodox belief, clarifying obscurities, drawing moral lessons, and dealing with such problems as these: Why did Christ allow himself to be tempted? Why are there only three temptations recorded? Did they correspond to those of Adam? Were they subjective or objective? Why did the Lord fast forty days? Why did he meet Satan's attacks by quoting scripture? Why did the devil choose these particular temptations? What led him to undertake the temptation in the first place? What does the ministry of the angels imply?

If the seventeenth-century reader turned from the commentaries to collections of homilies, volumes of sermons, biographies of Christ, or tracts on the temptation, he found the same questions raised and the same answers given. When he went to church, he heard them expounded from the pulpit. When he read a fictional or poetic account of the temptation like the one in Fletcher's *Christ's Victory and Triumph*, he saw that it was based on the accepted and familiar conception of the event. When he opened his copy of *Paradise Regained* in 1671, he must have expected to find the subject treated in conformity with the fixed principles established by the tradition.

It is the purpose of this study to determine how far *Paradise Regained* answered his expectations. That Milton knew the

xi

conventional views of the temptation current in his own day goes without saying: no educated or zealous Christian could have avoided knowing them, much less a man of Milton's great erudition and exhaustive knowledge of theology. He may have accepted, altered, or entirely rejected them. But he can hardly have sat down and reckoned up the simple possibilities of the Gospel narrative in the spirit of an Elizabethan dramatist wondering if this or that Italian legend could somehow be moulded into a likely play. He was, rather, in the position of a medieval poet writing a romance of courtly love or a modern author a novel about abnormal psychology: his subject was already defined in the terms of highly important technical studies well known to his audience.

In criticizing works of this particular type, it is always safest to begin where the writer himself begins—with the results of the technical studies. Even if he changes or discards them, the nature and direction of his rebellion are commonly determined by the very views against which he revolts and frequently inexplicable except in relation to them, while at the least we will be preserved from the absurdity of supposing he was revolting against views of a kind he never heard of, or denying principles which did not even exist in his time. But nothing we know of Milton suggests that he was any more likely to reject contemporary theology than his medieval predecessor the theory of *amour courtois* or his modern successor the discoveries of Freud or Jung. He was a man who united a profound independence of intellect with an equally profound love of traditional learning, and his first instinct always seems to have been to preserve and use every scrap of past authority as long as he could do so without either violating his reason or tampering with his conscience. We should expect him, therefore, simply on the face of things, to take the conventional views of the temptation into account and even to follow them as he saw fit, though he would certainly feel free to alter the most unquestioned if it did not happen to suit him. But we need not argue the point merely on the grounds of Milton's character. A. H. Gilbert has already observed that the poet's conception of the first temptation is identical with Calvin's.[1]

[1] A. H. Gilbert, "The Temptation in Paradise Regained," *JEGP* 15 (1916). 599-611.

Blakeney notes that Prudentius, like Milton, thought that Satan undertook the temptation to ascertain whether Christ was the Messiah or not;[2] and Merritt Hughes calls attention to the fact that the devil's disguise is similar to the one he adopts in Fletcher's *Christ's Victory and Triumph* and Bale's *Temptation of Our Lord*.[3] And with this evidence that Milton actually accepted and utilized parts of the tradition, it becomes more than ever necessary that we should fully investigate the whole.

For if he decided to treat his subject " as already defined in the terms of highly important technical studies well known to his audience," the fact gave him at least one great advantage: he could trust the audience to understand him. He did not have to clutter and weigh down his fiction with technical elucidation of what everybody knew already—a word, a sentence, the mere handling of a scene, would be enough to show his readers why the characters were speaking or behaving as they were. No doubt there were times when he deliberately tried to make himself absolutely clear. But even when he thought he was being explicit almost to tediousness, he could still hardly help counting to a certain extent on that common fund of knowledge he shared with his audience, and taking for granted some elementary assumption, some basic hypothesis, some point too ridiculously obvious to bring up or to dwell on. It would have been surprising if he had not: the amount of pure explanation in any good poem or novel usually varies in direct proportion to the amount of information a writer can safely assume on the part of his audience. This year, for instance, he would probably make a passing allusion to the Œdipus complex without defining it or even reflecting that thirty years ago it may have needed definition, and seventy years from now may need it again in the centennial edition of his collected works. When the same principle is applied not to a passing allusion, but to the whole system of ideas upon which the work itself is built, the consequences are very much more serious. The method remains satisfactory only while the opinions which form the book's frame of reference continue alive and in good standing, as they

---

[2] *Paradise Regained*, ed. E. H. Blakeney (London, 1932), p. 96.

[3] *Paradise Regained*, ed. M. Y. Hughes (New York, 1937), p. 419.

still are in the case of the modern novel about abnormal psychology. It is less satisfactory when those opinions are obsolete and have to be laboriously reconstructed for the proper training of the reader, as they do in the case of the medieval romance about courtly love. But what if they are not current, and not even obsolete, but simply and almost entirely forgotten, as they are in the case of *Paradise Regained?* How then is the audience to discriminate between the long speech of secondary importance and the key phrase casually introduced and briefly dismissed, merely to guide the initiated? What real evidence have they that the conclusions they draw are those which the author meant them to draw? What is to prevent them from misinterpreting scenes presented almost without comment, on the assumption that everyone would understand their significance?

In other words, it seems probable that unless we recover that lost frame of reference, we cannot hope fully to understand the poem, and may even be in grave danger of misunderstanding it completely. R. D. Miller, for example, considered it a sort of intellectual monstrosity, apparently because he assumed that anyone with sense would naturally interpret the Gospel narrative as the most advanced school of modern theology does: the presentation in symbolic terms of Christ's various efforts to decide by what line of action he could best carry out his mission.[4] Since the seventeenth-century conception of the temptation bears almost no resemblance to that of the modern school, Miller's castigation of *Paradise Regained* for its stupidity and lack of insight is entirely natural, but can hardly be described as fair. The critics who noted its affiliations with the work of Calvin, Prudentius, Fletcher, and Bale were wiser. But they merely touched briefly on isolated similarities, without linking their discoveries together, pushing their investigations further, and attempting to cover the whole field. And to comprehend either the tradition or the poem, it is necessary to make just that attempt.

In the first place, very few individual writers deal with every

[4] R. D. Miller, "Milton's Conception of the Temptation as Portrayed in *Paradise Regained*," *MLN* 15 (1900). 202-5. For a technical discussion of the modern view of the temptation, see for example, the *Abingdon Bible Commentary*, ed. Frederick Carl Eiselen, Edwin Lewis, and David G. Downey (New York and Nashville, 1929), pp. 959-60; 999; 1036; and for a work of fiction based upon that view, Gerald Heard, *A Dialogue in the Desert*. New York, 1942.

possible aspect of the temptation; they tend to discuss the points which interest them, and to neglect those which do not. Again, when there is more than one possible interpretation of the same point, they are inclined to choose one and ignore the other. Finally, they not infrequently present a point without treating it fully: for instance, a writer may observe that Christ's temptation resembled Adam's, but make no effort to carry out a detailed comparison of the two. Hence, we cannot assume that the work of a single exegete or homilist represents all that was thought or universally accepted.

On the other hand, commentators seldom or never stray outside the limits of established opinion, or offer purely personal or idiosyncratic views. There is nothing about the tradition more remarkable than the way its authorities keep within a limited circle of clearly defined themes or ideas. They are like children who have been given a certain number of blocks to play with: they select, and discard, and arrange in different patterns; but they always use the same blocks. Hence, while it is not possible to obtain a complete account of the tradition from any one writer, or even from any ten, it is possible to obtain it from any twenty.

For this very reason, I have made no attempt to determine the exact sources from which Milton drew his own conception of the tradition, or to confine myself to those which he demonstrably knew or could have known. The frequency with which their names appear in his prose suggests that he was familiar with the work of Ambrose, Augustine, Origen, Calvin, Bucer, Beza, Erasmus, Musculus, and Aretius, to name only a few; but even the fact that he owned or might have consulted a particular volume is no guarantee that he read a particular section of that volume or drew from it information that he might equally well have derived from a dozen other sources. All that can or need be established is the existence of a tradition so widespread and so consistent that a man even superficially acquainted with medieval and Renaissance theology could have hardly avoided learning it in its most complete form — and Milton's acquaintance with medieval and Renaissance theology was far from superficial. Some of the authorities available to him and to his audience have now either completely disappeared or were unobtainable at the time this study was written. But the group covered seems comprehensive enough to insure that no really important or familiar hypothesis has been wholly overlooked, and that, in the words of one seventeenth-century commentator, "enough may be collected out of them, to give a modest and sober minde convenient satisfaction." Taken together, they should certainly provide us with as much information as Milton had any right to expect of the average reader in his own day.

Chapter I

THE GOSPEL NARRATIVE

Only three of the Evangelists describe Christ's temptation: Mark, Luke, and Matthew. Mark sums it up in two verses:

And immediately [after the baptism] the spirit driveth him into the wilderness.

And he was there in the wilderness forty days, tempted of Satan; and was with the wild beasts; and the angels ministered unto him.[1]

Luke's account of the event is more elaborate:

And Jesus being full of the Holy Ghost returned from Jordan, and was led by the Spirit into the wilderness,

Being forty days tempted of the devil. And in those days he did eat nothing: and when they were ended, he afterward hungered.

And the devil said unto him, If thou be the Son of God, command this stone that it be made bread.

And Jesus answered him, saying, It is written, That man shall not live by bread alone, but by every word of God.

And the devil, taking him up into an high mountain, shewed unto him all the kingdoms of the world in a moment of time.

And the devil said unto him, All this power will I give thee, and the glory of them: for that is delivered unto me; and to whomsoever I will I give it.

If thou therefore wilt worship me, all shall be thine.

And Jesus answered and said unto him, Get thee behind me, Satan: for it is written, Thou shalt worship the Lord thy God, and him only shalt thou serve.

And he brought him to Jerusalem, and set him on a pinnacle of the temple, and said unto him, If thou be the Son of God, cast thyself down from hence:

For it is written, He shall give his angels charge over thee, to keep thee:

And in their hands they shall bear thee up, lest at any time thou dash thy foot against a stone.

And Jesus answering said unto him, It is said, Thou shalt not tempt the Lord thy God.

And when the devil had ended all the temptation, he departed from him for a season.[2]

Matthew's version is very like Luke's:

[1] Mark, 1: 12-13.　　　　　　[2] Luke, 4: 1-13.

Then was Jesus led up of the spirit into the wilderness to be tempted of the devil.

And when he had fasted forty days, and forty nights, he was afterwards an hungered.

And when the tempter came to him, he said, If thou be the Son of God, command that these stones be made bread.

But he answered and said, It is written, Man shall not live by bread alone, but by every word that proceedeth out of the mouth of God.

Then the devil taketh him up into the holy city, and setteth him on a pinnacle of the temple.

And saith unto him, If thou be the Son of God, cast thyself down: for it is written, He shall give his angels charge concerning thee: and in their hands they shall bear thee up, lest at any time thou dash thy foot against a stone.

Jesus said unto him, It is written again, Thou shalt not tempt the Lord thy God.

Again, the devil taketh him up into an exceeding high mountain, and showeth him all the kingdoms of the world, and the glory of them;

And saith unto him, All these things will I give thee, if thou wilt fall down and worship me.

Then saith Jesus unto him, Get thee hence, Satan: for it is written, Thou shalt worship the Lord thy God, and him only shalt thou serve.

Then the devil leaveth him, and, behold, angels came and ministered unto him.[3]

John's failure to treat the subject was not considered remarkable. As Origen pointed out, his Gospel was primarily concerned with Christ as Incarnate Word or God, and begins with an account of the Lord's divine origins instead of the elaborate Jewish genealogies that fill the first pages of Matthew and Luke. Since the temptation, like the genealogies, related only to the human nature of Jesus, it had no real place in John's work, and, like the genealogies, was discarded.[4]

The discrepancies between the versions of the temptation given by the other Evangelists constituted a more serious problem. In the first place, they differ as to the number of trials endured, and the length of time they lasted. Mark asserts that Jesus fasted and was tempted for forty days. Matthew, on the other hand, writes as if there were only three tempta-

---

[3] Matthew, 4: 1-11.
[4] Origen, *In Lucam Homiliae, Patr. Gr.* 13. col. 1876.

tions, all of which occurred after the forty days were over. Luke occupies an anomalous position between the two. What actual temptations he records are identical with those found in Matthew, and, like them, placed at the conclusion of the Lord's fast. He agrees with Mark, however, that Christ was tempted for forty days. But the Greek clause which the King James version renders as "led by the Spirit into the wilderness, *being forty days tempted of the devil*," can equally well be translated: "led by the Spirit into the wilderness for forty days, *and he was tempted of the devil*." [5] It was therefore possible to assume that Luke, like Matthew, thought that all the temptations came together at the end of the forty days. Even if this dubious hypothesis were accepted, however, it did not resolve the basic contradiction: it simply left Matthew and Luke against Mark instead of Mark and Luke against Matthew.

There were two ways of dealing with the difficulty. The easier was merely to ignore it: to accept the account given by the particular Evangelist one was working with at the moment, and say nothing of any other. Bede, for instance, states in his commentary on Mark that Christ was tempted all forty days; [6] but in his commentary on Matthew, he treats the forty days wholly as a period of fasting, and mentions no temptations except those actually authorized by his source.[7] And many theologians of the Middle Ages and the Renaissance followed the same practice.[8]

Others, however, attempted to reconcile the conflicting statements of Matthew, Mark, and Luke by suggesting that Christ

---

[5] This is the reading given by the Vulgate; by Erasmus (*Novum Instrumentum . . . Cum Annotationes* [Basel, 1516], p. 327); by Luca (*In Lucam Commentaria* [1606], *Script. Sacr. Cursus Compl.* 22. col. 527); and by Abraham Calovius (*Biblia Novi Testamenti Illustrata* [Francofurti ad Moenum, 1676], p. 30). Joachim Camerarius prefers the translation: "*where* he was tempted of the devil." (*Commentarii in Novum Foedus* [Cambridge, 1642], p. 27). Beza accepts the King James reading (*Annotationes in Novum Testamentum* [Cambridge, 1642], p. 167).

[6] Bede, *In Marci Evangelium Expositio, Patr. Lat.* 92. col. 139.

[7] Bede, *In Matthaei Evangelium Expositio, Patr. Lat.* 92. col. 18 ff.

[8] See for example: Jerome, *Commentarius in Evangelium Matthaei, Patr. Lat.* 26. col. 32 ff.; St. Gregory the Great, *XL Homiliarum in Evangelia, Patr. Lat.* 76. col. 1137 ff.; St. Bruno Astensius, *Commentaria in Matthaeum, Patr. Lat.* 165. col. 93 ff.; Cornelius Jansen, *In Lucam Commentaria* [1639], *Script. Sacr. Cursus Compl.* 22. col. 229 ff., M. Luther, *Sermon on Matt. 4:1-11* [1537], *Werke*, ed. J. F. K. Knaake, G. Kawerau, E. Thiele, and others (Weimar, 1883—), 45. 25 ff.; W. Musculus, *In Evangelium Matthaeum Commentarii* (Basel, 1544), p. 41 ff.

had undergone continual attacks from the devil throughout
his stay in the wilderness, but that there were only three which
the Evangelists had thought fit to preserve. Origen assumes
that the rest were left unwritten because they were greater
than the world could believe or endure.[9] Euthymius Zigabenus,
on the other hand, contends that the temptations which took
place during the forty days were comparatively insignificant:
sleepiness, gloominess, listlessness, and the like.[10] Much the
same conclusion was reached by Calvin, who makes no attempt
to identify the particular sins Satan urged Christ to commit,
but implies that they were slighter and more venial than the
ones which followed them:

Satan avoit assailli Christ quarante jours au paravent qu'il eust
faim: nous sachions que Satan veincu en plusieurs assaus, s'est
finalement rué furieusement, et de toute sa force, pour voir s'il
pourroit d'aventure veincre finalement celuy duquel il n'avoit peu
venir au bout.[11]

Knox, Thomas Taylor, Pareus, the authors of the *Dutch Annotations*, and other Renaissance theologians agree with Calvin
that the temptations of the forty days were mild in comparison
with those that came afterwards.[12] The inference is that the
three temptations actually recounted by the Evangelists were
given at length because they were the fiercest and the strongest,
while those which preceded them were not recognized by Matthew, or described by Mark and Luke, because they were not
considered sufficiently important to warrant so much attention.

[9] Origen, *In Lucam Homiliae*, col. 1874.

[10] Euthymius Zigabenus, *Commentarius in Quatuor Evangelia, Patr. Gr.* 129. col.
175. See also Thomas Bilson, *The Survey of Christs Sufferings for Mans Redemption* (London, 1604), p. 308; and William Perkins, *Satans Sophistrie Answered by
our Saviour Christ* (London, 1604), p. 25.

[11] J. Calvin, *La Concordance, qu'on Appelle Harmonie, Composée de Trois Evangelistes*, quoted by William Pringle in his translation of the *Commentarii in Quatuor
Evangelistas* (Edinburgh, 1846), 1.211. The *Concordance* is Calvin's French version of the *Commentarii*. The passage is not in the Latin original.

[12] J. Knox, *An Exposition Upon Christ's Temptations* [1583], *Works*, ed. D. Laing
(Edinburgh, 1855), 4.99; T. Taylor, *An Exposition of Christ's Temptations* (n. p.,
1618), p. 47; D. Pareus, *In S. Matthaei Evangelia Commentarius* (Oxford, 1631),
p. 65; *Dutch Annotations*, trans. Theodore Haak (London, 1637), 2. sig. L4r; J.
Udall, *The Combate Betweene Christ, and the Deuill* (London, 1589), sig. B5v;
John Trapp, *A Commentary or Exposition upon all the Books of the New Testament*
(London, 1656), pp. 31, 384; Cornelius à Lapide, *Commentarii in IV. Evangelia*
[16—?] (Antuerpiae, 1712), p. 99; T. Fuller, *A Comment on Christ's Temptations
Delivered in XII Sermons* (London, 1652), p. 34.

John Lightfoot, on the other hand, seems to be of the opinion that the difference between the recorded and the unrecorded temptations was one of form rather than of kind: that Satan tried for forty days to tempt Christ as he did other men, secretly, by "injecting sinful suggestions into him," [13] but finding that Christ's mind was not susceptible of sinful suggestions, he was forced in the end to appear in a visible form and try to conquer him by direct persuasion. Lancelot Andrewes, too, thought the unrecorded temptations were similar to the recorded ones, but assumed that they were not enumerated because the three we have represent "a brief abridgment of all." [14]

Milton, however, preferred to solve the problem by the simpler method of conforming to one Gospel and ignoring the others. In *Paradise Regained*, he follows the lead of Matthew: Satan appears in the wilderness and the temptations begin only at the expiration of the forty days, during which Christ has not been molested. This need not mean that Milton was unaware of the difference between Matthew's account and that of his fellow-evangelists, or ignorant of the efforts that had been made to reconcile the three, or inclined to think that Matthew's version of events was truer than that of Luke or Mark. But whatever he may have thought of Matthew's version as a theologian, it was the one most likely to appeal to a poet with a narrative to write, and a critic with a predilection for classic form. The grouping of the temptations together at the end of the forty days prevented any diffusion of energy and interest, centered the attention of the reader on the main issue, and, above all, gave the central situation that special quality of unity or strength which results from the compression of incident within a limited period of time. Even to imply that the major temptations were merely the last of many would entail a certain loss of coherence and effectiveness for which the slight gain in historical accuracy could hardly compensate.

[13] J. Lightfoot, *A Harmony of the Gospels* [1654], *Works*, ed. J. R. Pitman (London, 1822-25), 3. 42. See also R. Ward, *Theologicall Questions Upon St. Matthewe* (London, 1640), p. 96; and S. Cradock, *The Harmony of the Four Evangelists* (London, 1670), p. 39.

[14] L. Andrewes, *Seven Sermons on the Temptation* [1592], *Ninety-Six Sermons*, ed. J. Parkinson (Oxford, 1841-43), p. 496.

But while Milton agrees that there were no temptations prior to the ones described by Matthew, he introduces, within the framework of Matthew's temptations, two new episodes which he invented for himself: the banqueting scene that precedes the offer of the kingdoms, and the storm scene which follows it. It is not unlikely that when he composed them, he expected his readers to remember the old hypothesis that there had been many unrecorded temptations, and to feel that he had a certain amount of authority for bringing into his narrative two which were not directly based on any specifically mentioned in the Gospels. There is, however, no need to make too much of this possibility: everything we know of Milton's character suggests that he was quite capable of interpolating any supplementary temptations he thought necessary on no one's authority but his own.

The only other serious discrepancy between the accounts of the Evangelists was the difference in the order of the temptations listed by Matthew and Luke. Matthew places the temptation of bread first, the temptation of the tower second, and the temptation of the kingdoms third; Luke places the temptation of bread first, the temptation of the kingdoms second, and the temptation of the tower third.

The theologians of the Middle Ages and the Renaissance met this new difficulty very much as they had met the first one. Some simply followed the order given by the particular Evangelist they were working with, and disregarded the other. Others acknowledged and attempted to solve the problem. Those who did generally came to the conclusion that the order in Matthew was the historically correct one. In the first place, the temptations as he gives them are arranged in an " orderly consequent," linked by the significant word *then* instead of the vague *and* used by Luke, which implies that the latter had no clear and fixed time-scheme in mind.[15] Again, Matthew places the temptation of the tower where it logically belongs, immediately after the temptation of bread. For the one obviously grew out of

[15] T. Taylor, p. 155. See also Lightfoot, p. 41; Lapide, p. 103; John Mayer, *A Commentarie upon the New Testament* (London, 1631), p. 81; J. Maldonatus, *In Quatuor Evangelistas Commentarii* (Moguntiae, 1622-24), col. 88; and M. Chemnitius, *Libri Tres Harmoniae Evangelicae* (Francofurti ad Moenum, 1600), p. 33.

the other: the first showed Satan that Christ had unlimited confidence in God's protecting care, so he devoted the second to persuading him to misplace or abuse that confidence.[16] Finally, in Matthew, the devil immediately ceases his attacks when Christ commands him to do so at the temptation of the kingdoms.[17] It is obviously more natural and fitting to suppose that Satan submitted than it is to assume that he went on tempting Christ in the face of a positive order to stop.[18] Furthermore, as Richard Baxter points out, "when it cometh to blasphemous and atheistical temptations, Satan should be driven away, and no longer disputed with and endured." [19]

But if the order given by Matthew is the right one, why should Luke have altered it? William Perkins suggested that he was less careful of the order than Matthew because he was more concerned with relating all the facts than arranging them in their proper sequence: "*Luke* in penning of the words and deeds of Christ, sets them downe as the Spirit of God directed him, not regarding precisely the time when they were done, but sometime setting that first which was done last: but *Mathew* he sets them down in order as they were performed by our Saviour Christ." [20] Lightfoot supposed that "Luke, for our better observing of this parallel [between the temptations of Christ and Adam] hath laid the order of these temptations answerable to the order of those." [21] Luca, on the other hand, thought it possible that the order in Luke originally

---

[16] T. Taylor, pp. 155-56; Lapide, p. 103; Chemnitius, p. 46; Daniel Dyke, *Two Treatises* (London, 1635), p. 273; John Downame, *The Christian Warfare* (London, 1612), p. 63; Johann Piscator, *Analysis Logica Libri S. Lucae* (London, 1597), p. 49; Christopher Blackwood, *Expositions and Sermons upon the Ten First Chapters of Matthew* (London, 1659), p. 105.

[17] T. Taylor, p. 156; Pareus, p. 67; Piscator, p. 49; Dyke, p. 273; Chemnitius, p. 33; and John Diodate, *Pious and Learned Annotations upon the Holy Bible* (London, 1651), sec. sig. A3ʳ.

[18] Luca, col. 536. Euthymius Zigabenus (col. 179) and Luca (col. 536) note that Luke's "Get thee behind me!" has the force of "Desist!" or "Out of my sight!" Cf. Erasmus, *In Novum Testamentum Annotationes* (Basel, 1522), pp. 21-22.

[19] Richard Baxter, *A Paraphrase on the New Testament* [1685] (London, 1810), p. 6.

[20] Perkins, pp. 54-55. See also Euthymius Zigabenus, col. 179; Dyke, p. 273; Mayer, p. 81. Lightfoot agrees, but adds that it was unnecessary for Luke to trouble himself about the order because it had already been fixed by Matthew (p. 41).

[21] Lightfoot, p. 42.

corresponded to the one in Matthew, and that the present discrepancy between the two is the work of some careless or inefficient scribe, who in copying transposed the second and third temptations because both begin with the same phrase: *Et duxit illum.*[22]

Other theologians, however, raised the question only to decide that it was too idle and unimportant to warrant attention. As Calvin put it, in his harmony of the Gospels:

> Non magni interest quod Lucas secundo loco tentationem recitat quae in postremum locum a Matthaeo rejicitur. neque enim propostum Evangelistis fuit historiae filum sic contexere ut temporis rationem semper exacte servarent: sed rerum summas colligere, ut in speculo vel tabula proponerent quae de Christo maxime utilia sunt cognitu. Tenere ergo sufficiat, Christum tribus modis fuisse tentatum. Quod autem vel secundum vel tertium fuerit certamen, non est cur anxie laboremus.[23]

But then, having made his point, Calvin immediately goes on to add: "In expositione sequar Matthaei contextum." In other words, when it became necessary to make a positive choice between the order in Matthew and the order in Luke, it was the order in Matthew he selected and used.

This in itself would not be particularly significant if so many other writers confronted by the same alternative did not make the same choice. An exegete or a homilist composing a commentary or a book of sermons on the gospel of Luke usually followed the order of temptations authorized by his source. But throughout the Middle Ages and the Renaissance, it seems to have been customary, almost obligatory, to use the Matthew order in every work which left the decision in the hands of the author: a harmony of the Evangelists, a life of Christ, a mystery play, a poem, an "exposition" of the temptation, a sermon or a group of sermons which did not form part of a large collection specifically based on Luke. *Paradise Regained* is the only exception to the rule that I have so far encountered.[24]

---

[22] Luca, col. 536. See also Chemnitius, pp. 32-33.

[23] John Calvin, *Commentarii in Quatuor Evangelistas: Quorum Tres Priores in Formam Harmoniae Sunt Digesti* (Amstelodami, 1667), p. 52. See also Martin Bucer, *Enarrationum in Evangelia Matthaei, Marci, & Lucae* (Argentorati, 1527), fol. 100ᵛ; and Augustine Marlorate, *A Catholike and Ecclesiastical Exposition of the Holy Gospel after S. Mathewe*, trans. Thomas Tymme (London, 1570), p. 62.

[24] See for example: Caedmon [?], *Christ and Satan*. Ed. Merrel D. Chubb. New

As long as there was a fixed system of iconography, the Matthew order apparently dominated art as well. *The Guide for Painters*, a handbook on technique and iconography compiled for the Byzantine school, directs its readers to place the temptation of bread first, the temptation of the tower second, and the temptation of the kingdoms third in any representation of the subject.[25] Western artists commonly follow the same rule.[26]

During the Renaissance, however, the stable iconography of the Middle Ages broke down, and artists began to depict the temptations in whatever order they pleased. They usually portray all three: one in the foreground, one in the middle ground, and one in the background. Sometimes this arrangement is clearly intended to show the chronological sequence of the temptations, since Satan appears flying away or plunging down through the air in a state of collapse in the background scene.[27]

Haven, 1925; Aelfric, *Homilies*, in *The Homilies of the Anglo-Saxon Church.* Ed. Benjamin Thorpe. London, 1844; *Twelfth Century Homilies.* Ed. A. O. Balfour. London, 1909; *Ludus Coventriae.* Ed. K. S. Block. London, 1922; Andrewes, *Seven Sermons on the Temptation*; Knox, *An Exposition Upon Christ's Temptation*; Giles Fletcher, *Christ's Victory and Triumph*, in *Poetical Works.* Ed. F. S. Boas. Cambridge, 1908; Henry More, *The Life and Doctrine of our Saviour Jesus Christ.* Gant, 1656; Alexander Ross, *Christiados.* Rotterdam, 1653; Marcus Vida, *The Christiad.* Trans., Edward Granan. London, 1771; Robert Allen, *The Doctrine of the Gospel.* London, 1606; etc.

[25] *The Guide for Painters*, translated from the Greek by P. Durand, and reprinted in A. N. Didron, *Christian Iconography*, translated and completed by Margaret Stokes (London, 1886), 2. 302-3. The *Guide*, in its present form, dates only from the Renaissance, but is a copy of an older manuscript compiled by the monk Dionysius from the works of the celebrated painter Manuel Panselinos, who flourished in the twelfth century (*ibid.*, 2. 190).

[26] See for example: two windows at Chartres Cathedral (12th to 13th centuries); Illustrated ms. (10th century), *Gospel Book of Otto*, fol. 52, in the Cathedral Treasury at Aachen, reproduced in Beissel, *Hs. Kaisers Otto* (1886), pl. 7; Miniature in the Boxall-Coleridge-Richee manuscript of *Speculum Humanae Salvationis* (14th century), ed. M. R. James (Oxford, 1926), p. 22.

See also an enamel on a reliquary at Orvieto: Cath., Assunta (1338), reproduced in *Diana* 4 (1929), pl. 18 opp. p. 26; Fresco at Brinay, Ch., Aignan, Choir (12th century), reproduced in *Gaz. B. A.* 56 (1914), figs. 227 and 229; Duccio, two panels from the section of his *Maesta* depicting the temptations of the kingdoms and the temptation of the tower (c. 1311). None of these show a complete temptation with three scenes: the first two give merely the temptation of the kingdoms. But the fact that all portray Satan fleeing and the angels approaching proves that the artists are following the order in Matthew. Detzel says that Western artists frequently confined themselves to the final scenes of a subject when they lacked the space to treat it fully (*Christliche Iconographie* [Breisgau, 1894], 1. 256).

[27] See Plate II.

In that case, the artist may follow either the order in Matthew or the order in Luke: he may place the temptation of the tower in the middle ground and the temptation of the kingdoms (with the departure of Satan) in the background; or the temptations of the kingdoms in the middle ground, and the temptation of the tower (with the departure of Satan) in the background.[28] Sometimes, on the other hand, the placing of the episodes seems to bear no relation to the chronological sequence of the temptations: the temptation of the tower occupies the background, and the temptation of the kingdoms (with the departure of Satan), the middle ground, where it obviously does not belong.[29] As a result, when an artist does not show Satan in flight at one of the temptations, it is impossible to tell whether he intends to present the scenes in a chronological sequence or not.[30]

How well Milton knew the iconography of his own day is an open question. There is no record that he ever showed much interest in art, even when he had his sight and was travelling in Italy, with the achievements of the Renaissance on every side. Furthermore, it is natural to suppose that by the time he composed *Paradise Regained*, twenty years of blindness had seriously impaired his visual memory. But he may once have seen and half-consciously remembered some contemporary print or woodcut which showed the temptations in the Luke order, with Satan plunging headlong from the tower at the last

[28] Jerome Wierix (two prints after Bernardino Passeri, in the Baltimore Museum of Art, 1680-81), and a woodcut illustrating the *Bibel Froschzauer* (1551), p. clxxxiv, both follow the order in Matthew. In a woodcut of the temptation used to illustrate "*Cranmer's*" *Catechism* (1548), reproduced by Burton in his edition (Oxford, 1829), p. 167; an engraving by Meister LCz, reproduced by Elfried Bock, *Geschichte der Graphischen Kunst* (Berlin, 1930), p. 183; and an engraving of uncertain date in the extra-illustrated Kitto Bible in the Huntingdon Library, the artists follow the order in Luke. See Plate II. Since the illustrations in the Kitto Bible were cut out of old Bibles or religious works, it is usually impossible to date or place them with accuracy, but all I cite belong to the period under discussion.

[29] Five woodcuts and engravings of uncertain date in the extra-illustrated Kitto Bible in the Huntington Library. See Plate VIII.

[30] See Jan Van Londerseel, *Landscape with the Temptation of Christ*, after David Verick-Boons (1578-1629), print in the Baltimore Museum of Art; George Yate, engraving used to illustrate the 1640 edition of Giles Fletcher, *Christ's Victory and Triumph*, reproduced by Boas in *Works*, 1. 44; five woodcuts and engravings of uncertain date in the extra-illustrated Kitto Bible in the Huntington Library: see Plates I, IV, and VI. In Plate VI, the Matthew order is used; all the others follow Luke.

one—perhaps a print or woodcut used to illustrate a Bible he was accustomed to pore over as a child, at a time when such a picture might permanently impress his imagination. It is not an uncommon experience to find that one's conception of a scene like the trial at Vanity Fair or Christ's blessing of the little children has been forever fixed by the dog-eared picture in the nursery *Pilgrim's Progress* or the stained-glass window in the local Sunday School. And it is noteworthy that no other writer that I know of states that Satan *fell* after his final defeat: they simply say that he " departed " or that he " fled away." [31] Artists, however, frequently depict him reeling or cowering away from the brink of the mountain or the tower in such a state of collapse that he looks very much as if he were actually falling.[32] But I do not wish to labor the point. There was no reason why Milton should not have picked up the " fall " motif from *Christ's Victory and Triumph*, in which the allegorical figure of Presumption "tombles headlong"[33] from the tower at the end of the second temptation. Or he may have worked it out for himself as a sort of pendant to the original fall from heaven in *Paradise Lost*, with which the angels specifically equate Satan's defeat at the close of the poem:

> True Image of the Father . . . still expressing
> The Son of God, with Godlike force indu'd
> Against th'Attempter of thy Fathers Throne,
> And Thief of Paradise; *him long of old*
> *Thou didst debel, and down from Heav'n cast*
> *With all his Army*, now thou hast aveng'd
> Supplanted *Adam*, and by vanquishing
> Temptation, hast regain'd lost Paradise
> And frustrated the conquest fraudulent.[34]

Or it may have struck Milton as dramatically appropriate that the devil should fall " whence he stood to see his victim fall."[35] On the other hand, the Luke order and the "fall" motif occur so frequently in art and so seldom in literature that I think we must at least reckon with the possibility that he may have been working consciously or unconsciously under the influence of the pictorial tradition.

---

[31] See for example: Calvin, *Commentarii*, p. 53; Fletcher, 1.56; Jansen, col. 546; Ross, p. 258; Dyke, p. 356.
[32] See Plates VIII and IX.
[33] Fletcher, 1.49.
[34] *P.R.*, 4.597-609. Italics mine.
[35] *P.R.*, 4.571.

It is very unlikely, however, that any vague recollection of a Renaissance print or woodcut would be enough *in itself* to offset the whole weight of the literary tradition, which, as we have seen, was strongly prepossessed in favor of the order given by Matthew. Milton must have known that that order was almost invariably used by writers who had any choice in the matter, and generally considered the historically correct one by theologians who dealt with the question. While it may not have been heretical to prefer and follow the order in Luke, it was certainly unusual — so unusual that I cannot believe Milton would have thus flown in the face of opinion and precedent merely to gratify a whimsical preference for some picture he may once have seen and enjoyed. At the very best, his memory of the picture can have been only one of many contributing causes which finally led him to reject the order in Matthew. The discussion of those causes properly belongs to the analysis of his temptation of the tower.

CHAPTER II

THE EXALTED MAN

In Book One, Chapter Fourteen of *The Christian Doctrine*, Milton writes that though

> the two natures [divine and human] constitute one Christ, . . . it sometimes happens . . . that what properly belongs to the compound nature of Christ, is attributed to one of his natures only . . . Scripture . . . frequently distinguishes what is peculiar to his human nature. Acts ii. 30. "of the fruit of the loins of David, according to the flesh." See also Rom. ix. 5. I Pet. iii. 18. "being put to death in the flesh," that is to say, being affected chiefly and most visibly in his human nature.[1]

In the following chapter, he repeats that when Christ offered himself as a sacrifice for the sins of the world, he offered himself "more particularly in his human nature, as many passages of Scripture expressly indicate."[2] And in Chapter Sixteen he speaks again of the Passion as an act performed "conspicuously" "'in the likeness of sinful flesh,'" and equates it with other occasions of the same kind: the circumcision, the flight into Egypt, the manual labor, the childhood subject to Mary and Joseph, the baptism, and "the persecutions, insults, and dangers which he underwent." With the rest he lists the temptation. All resulted from "THE HUMILIATION OF CHRIST . . . that state in which UNDER HIS CHARACTER OF GOD-MAN HE VOLUNTARILY SUBMITTED HIMSELF TO THE DIVINE JUSTICE, AS WELL IN LIFE AS IN DEATH, FOR THE PURPOSE OF UNDERGOING ALL THINGS REQUISITE TO ACCOMPLISH OUR REDEMPTION."[3]

In other words, to redeem man, it was necessary for the Son to take on man's nature and humble himself to undergo on man's behalf, and as man, everything of which that nature made him susceptible: immaturity, bodily pain, toil, peril, temptation, death. Hence, events which relate to immaturity, bodily pain, toil, peril, temptation, and death affect him "chiefly and most visibly in his human nature," since what

---

[1] John Milton, *Complete Works*, ed. F. A. Patterson (New York, 1931-38), 4. 279-81.

[2] *Ibid.*, 4. 293. [3] *Ibid.*, 4. 303-5.

they impose on him is never experienced by pure divinity, and never swept away by the exertion of his power, but endured in the character proper to the state he has assumed.

In thus making the temptation an event carried out *quasi homo* for the redemption of mankind, Milton was in agreement with a long line of theologians, of both the Middle Ages and the Renaissance, Catholic and Protestant alike. St. Ambrose, for instance, asks pertinently why the Lord should have taken on flesh, unless he wished to suffer temptation like any other human being, and by overcoming it show his followers how they too might do so:

Suscepit carnem, ut quasi homo vinceret, qui homines erudiret. Quid mihi prodesset, si quasi Deus exerta potestate divinitatem suam tantummodo inviolabilem demonstrasset? Aut cur susciperat carnem, nisi ut tentari se naturae atque infirmitatis meae conditione pateretur? Tentari debuit, compati mihi debuit, ut scirem quemadmodum tentatus vincerem, compassus evaderem.[4]

Cassiodorus writes that it was entirely fitting that Christ's human nature should have been tested and proved by temptation:

Natura enim humanitatis a Domino assumpta probatur esse, non culpa; sed tamen ipsem fortem sustinuit tentatorem, quia carnem nostrae fragilitatis assumpsit; nec aliter fieri potuit ut jus suum exitium juste perderet, nisi ad vite pervenisset auctorem.[5]

And St. Hilary carefully points out that *only* his human nature was so tested:

Christus ut homo primum probatus, deinde cognitus. Non confundenda autem persona divinitatis et corporis est. Omnis enim nunc in exordio ex persona ejus hominis, quem assumpsit, oratio est. *Probasti me, et cognovisti me.* Probatus est, ut cognosceretur: quia posterior est probatione cognitio. . . . In deserto agit, tentationi diaboli subjicitur, seseque nunc in fastigium templi, nunc in excelsum montem patitur efferri. Contumeliae itaque se injuriae tam gravis dedit, dum in deserto est, dum conditione tentationis illuditur, dum elevari potest in templum atque montem. Sed tentationum probationem, agnoscentis testimonium non reliquit. . . . Homo tentatur, homo circumfertur: sed post haec angeli ministrant.[6]

Bale, like Ambrose, says of Christ:

---

[4] St. Ambrose, *De Fide, Patr. Lat.* 16. col. 603.

[5] Cassiodorus, *Expositio in Psalterium, Patr. Lat.* 70. cols. 411-12.

[6] St. Hilary, *Tractatus in CXXXVIII Psalmum, Patr. Lat.* 9. cols. 795-96. Hilary, like Milton, cites the passion, the baptism, and the temptation together as signal

In mannys frayle nature, ye have conquerred the enmye,
That man over hym, shuld alwayes have vycoorye; [7]

while Pareus declares that the chief reason why the Lord
undertook the temptation can be found in Hebrews 2:17:
"Wherefore in all things it behooved him to be made like unto
his brethren, that he might be a merciful and faithful high
priest in things pertaining to God, to make reconciliation for
the sins of the people." [8] Or, as Udall puts it, "he tooke upon
him our nature, to the end that in the same he might overcome, (in which we are conquered of Satan, when he is encountered onely of our owne power) so that it is not only no
straunge thing, that he was tempted, but a thing most needfull
for our benefite." [9] And Maldonatus, in a splendid figure of
speech, pictures Christ laying aside the defenses of his Godhead
and going out to fight against Satan in all the nakedness of
humanity: "Arma quodāmodo divinitatis ponit, & quasi nudus
et inermis homo contra luctatorū morem esuriens in arenam
descendit." [10]

The theologians, however, were careful to point out that
Christ's susceptibility to temptation did not detract in the least
from his glory, his innocence, or his perfection, since, as Bede
explains, "ejus mentem delectatio peccati non momordit." [11]
The problem of how a being could be absolutely pure and yet
susceptible of temptation was, according to Marlorate,

no doubt at all, if we call to mynde the whole and perfect nature
of Adam, in whome although the Image of God did shyne, yet
nevethelesse, he was subiecte to temptations.[12]

Supplementary evidence confirming and strengthening the
view that Christ underwent the temptation as a man was found

instances of Christ's humanity. He also notes that each was followed by some
miracle or divine recognition of his supernatural origin and nature. Jeremy Taylor
makes the same point, but lists the birth, the circumcision, the flight into Egypt,
and the presentation as well as the passion, baptism, and temptation (*The Life of
Christ* [London, 1657], p. 542).

[7] J. Bale, *The Temptation of our Lord* [1538] (London, 1909), sig. E4ʳ.
[8] Pareus, p. 64.   [9] Udall, sig. B4ᵛ.   [10] Maldonatus, cols. 86-7.
[11] Bede, *In Matthaei Evangelium Expositio, Patr. Lat.*, 92. col. 19. See also St.
Thomas Aquinas, *Summa Theologica*, ed. Nicolai, Sylvii, Billuart, and C.-J. Drioux
(n. p., 1868), pars 3, quaest. 41, art. 1.
[12] Marlorate, p. 58. See also Calvin, *Commentarii*, p. 51; Udall, sig. B4ᵛ; Dyke,
p. 218; Perkins, p. 17; Lapide, p. 101.

in the Gospel narrative itself. In the first place, all three Evangelists say that he went into the wilderness under the guidance of the Spirit; and it was only " as tuiching his humane and manlie nature "[13] that he required direction or control. Again, he hungered when the forty days of fasting were over, to show that he shared the common infirmities of that nature.[14] Furthermore, the fast itself was similar to those undertaken by other men before they went to their people with some new revelation from God:

As Moses fasted forty days at the institution of the law [Exodus 24:18], and Elias forty at the restoration [I Kings 19:8], so Christ here. And because He came but in the shape of a servant, He would not take upon Him above His fellow-servants. Contrary to our times, wherein a man is accounted nobody except he can have a quirk above his fellows.[15]

And since Moses and Elijah had survived so long a period without food, Christ could do the same without calling his humanity into question: " he would not exceed the fasts of *Moses* and *Elias*; some think it was that Satan might not suspect him to be greater than they; *Theophylact, Euthymius*, lest otherwise, saith *Chrysostom* . . . his assumption of flesh, should seem incredible." [16]

---

[13] Knox, 4. 99. See also Luca, col. 534; Euthymius Zigabenus, col. 910; Baxter, p. 5; Abraham Woodhead, *An Historical Narration of the Life and Death of our Lord Jesus Christ* (Oxford, 1685), p. 108; Perkins, p. 7: " Christ as he is man is led and guided by the Spirit; but as he is God, he doth guide and send his Spirit."

[14] St. Hilary, *Commentarius in Matthaeum, Patr. Lat.* 9. col. 929; Walafridus Strabus, *Expositio in Quatuor Evangelia, Patr. Lat.* 114. col. 869; Luca, col. 531; J. Taylor, p. 542; Pareus, p. 65; Lapide, p. 101; Chemnitius, p. 37; Fuller, p. 29.

[15] Andrewes, p. 492. See also Jansen, col. 528; St. Jerome, col. 32; Knox, p. 101. Rabanus Maurus (*Commentaria in Matthaeum, Patr. Lat.* 107. col. 779) suggests that Christ followed the example of Moses and Elijah to show that he intended to make no break with the law and the prophets. St. Ambrose (*Expositionis in Lucam, Patr. Lat.* 15. cols. 1700-1) not only connects the fast with those of Moses and Elijah, but detects mystical significance in the number forty; for example, the Jews wandered in the wilderness forty years, and the earth was flooded for forty days. For similar discussions of the allegorical implications of " forty," see Walafridus Strabus, *Expositio*, col. 869; Jansen, cols. 528-30; Pseudo-Jerome, *Expositio Quatuor Evangeliorum, Patr. Lat.* 26. col. 558. As an example of how far such speculations could be carried, see St. Bruno Astensius (col. 93), who writes that the number represents the combination of the new law with the old: the four gospels multiplied by the ten commandments.

[16] *Assembly's Annotations* (London, 1651), 2. sig. J5ʳ. The references given are from Theophylactus, *Enarratio in Evangelium Lucae* (*Patr. Gr.* 123. col. 746); Euthymius Zigabenus (col. 174); and St. John Chrysostom, *Homiliae in Matthaeum*

Finally, Christ did not make use of his divine power to drive
the devil away or beat off his attacks, but overcame them as
every human being should: "per continentiam . . . per con-
temptum divitiarum . . . per fidem,"[17] and by falling back on
the authority of Scripture. As St. Leo the Great puts it:

Vicit enim adversarium ut audistis, testimoniis legis, non potestate
virtutis; ut hoc ipso et hominem plus honoraret, et adversarium
plus puniret, cum hostis generis humani non quasi a Deo jam, sed
quasi ab homine vinceretur.[18]

St. Gregory the Great adds that by his patience, courtesy, and
reliance on the Word of God, the Lord set his followers an
example which they would do well to remember when dealing
with the wicked.[19] True, he lost his temper and sharply rebuked
Satan at the temptation of the kingdoms; but, as St. Thomas
Aquinas explains, his anger on that occasion was entirely
proper, since it shows us that while we ought to take personal
injuries quietly, we should never suffer the Deity to be so
dishonored and insulted.[20]

But though the temptation was of necessity a trial of Christ's
humanity, his divinity may not have gone altogether without
acknowledgment. At the end of the trial, when the devil leaves
him, angels appear to minister to him; and by this act of sub-
mission (many authorities argued) they confessed him to be
their supreme Lord. St. Gregory the Great, for instance, writes:

Homo est quem diabolus tentat, et idem ipse Deus est cui ab
angelis ministratur. Cognoscamus igitur in eo naturam nostram,
quia nisi hunc diabolus hominem cerneret, non tentaret. Veneremur
in illo divinitatem suam, quia nisi super omnia Deus existeret ei
nullo modo angeli ministrarent.[21]

(Patr. Gr. 57. col. 209). See also Walafridus Strabus, Expositio, col. 869; Fuller,
p. 29; Edward Leigh, Annotations upon All the New Testament Philological and
Theologicall (London, 1650), p. 8.

[17] St. Ambrose, De Fide, col. 603.

[18] St. Leo the Great, Sermones, Patr. Lat. 54. col. 265. See also Assembly's
Annotations, 2. sig. A4ʳ; Ward, p. 101; Richard Capel, Tentations: Their Nature,
Danger, Cure (London, 1636), p. 170; Downame, pp. 61-62; Franciscus Junius,
Sacrorum Parallelorum Libri Tres (London, 1588), p. 35.

[19] St. Gregory the Great, col. 1136.

[20] St. Thomas Aquinas, Summa, pars 3, quaest. 41, art. 4. Falling down and
worshipping the devil would, of course, have been a direct repudiation of God
Himself. See also J. Taylor, p. 152, and Baxter, p. 6. Cf. Chapter I, p. 7.

[21] St. Gregory the Great, col. 1136. See also Pseudo-Jerome, col. 559; Rabanus

Or, as Thomas Manton elaborates the point in the seventeenth century:

As Christs humiliation and humane nature was to be manifested by the devils comming to him, and tempting Assaults; so the honour of his divine Nature by the Ministry of Angels, lest his temptations should seem to derogate from his Glory. When we read the story of his Temptations, how he was tempted in all parts like us, we might seem to take scandal, as if he were a mere man; therefore his humiliation is counter-ballanced with the special honour done to him; he was tempted as man, but as God ministered unto by Angels.[22]

Other theologians, however, were more inclined to think the ministry of the angels designed simply to show Christ's followers that if they overcame temptation, as he had, they would be praised and tended by the heavenly host, as he was.[23] This view of the question had the merit of providing the exegete with an excellent opportunity to bring the text home to the individual Christian; but Lapide criticizes the hypothesis sharply on the ground that it makes the Lord no better than his disciples: " ut Angeli Christo inseruierint sicut aliis Sanctis, anathema dicit eis, qui volunt Angelos ad Christum descendisse, eique ministrasse tamquam amico & domestico Dei, non tamquam creatori & Domino suo." [24] Perkins and Manton, however, who regarded the ministry as a tribute to the Incarnate God, add that the angels will likewise minister to us, but avoid any suggestion of self-contradiction by explaining that they serve us only as we are members of Christ's mystical body,

---

Maurus, *In Matthaeum*, col. 786; Walafridus Strabus, *Expositio*, col. 870; Bede, *In Matthaei Evangelium Expositio*, col. 20; St. Ambrose, *De Fide*, col. 596; *Assembly's Annotations*, 2. sig. A4ᵛ; Perkins, p. 136; J. Taylor, p. 542; T. Taylor, p. 402.

[22] Thomas Manton, *Christs Temptation and Transfiguration Practically Explained and Improved* (London, 1685), p. 186.

[23] See for example Chrysostom, col. 213; Euthymius Zigabenus, col. 182; Theophylactus, *Enarratio in Evangelium Matthaei*, *Patr. Gr.* 123. cols. 182-3; Pareus, p. 69; Bucer, fol. 103ʳ; Dyke, pp. 357-8; P. Hieronymus Xavier, *Historia Christi Persice Conscriptus*, ed. and trans. Ludovicus de Dieu (Lugduni Batavorun, ex offica Elseviriana, 1639), pp. 133-34; Johann Wild, *In Sacro Sanctum Iesu Christi Domini Nostri Evangelium Secundum Matthaeum* (Paris, 1564), fol. 60ᵛ. St. Hilary gives this note on the text in his *Commentarius in Matthaeum* (col. 931), but in his *Tractatus in CXXXVIII Psalmum* (col. 795-96), he implies rather that the ministry is to be considered an acknowledgment of Christ's divinity. Cf. above, pp. 14-15.

[24] Lapide, p. 108.

and one with him.[25] The commentators who stated merely
that we too will be comforted as our Lord was may have shared
the assumption made by Perkins and Manton without seeing
any necessity for stating it explicitly. On the other hand, they
may have felt that up to the very end Christ was still behaving
wholly as a human being, who receives assistance from heaven
as a privilege rather than as a right.

It was also somewhat difficult to determine the precise extent
to which Christ's divinity remained dormant during the temptation itself. Many medieval and Renaissance authorities write
as if they thought that while he deliberately surrendered one
part of his nature to hunger and the blandishments of the
devils, he retained full knowledge and control of the situation.
Among Protestant theologians, however, there seems to have
been a marked tendency to fight shy of this hypothesis whenever it threatened to make Christ's trial less than complete.
Apparently they reasoned that since he is said to have been
tempted "in all points like as we are," [26] he must have been
denied any special advantages of prescience or power which
might give the ungodly occasion to argue that his temptations
were noticeably easier to bear than our own. For instance,
whereas Chrysostom observes that Christ himself forbade the
angels to come on the scene before they did, lest the devil
should be frightened away before the completion of the trial,[27]
Calvin and Marlorate prefer to argue that, though we must
not think

that Christ at any tyme, was forsaken of the angels: but *that there
might be tyme and place geuen to the temptation*, the grace of God
for a while (though it were present with him) was hid from hym
in respect of the flesh, according to ye sence and felinge thereof.[28]

Again, Francis Luca declares that Christ hungered simply
because he willed that he should do so:

[25] Perkins, p. 136; Manton, p. 186. See also T. Taylor (p. 142), who writes that
the angels served Christ out of " dutie," but us only as " creatures of charge . . .
by special commission and direction from him." Much the same distinction is made
in *Twelfth Century Homilies*, p. 105.

[26] Hebrews 4:15.

[27] Chrysostom, col. 213. See also Euthymius Zigabenus, col. 182, and Lapide,
p. 577.

[28] Marlorate, p. 66. Italics mine. The passage is a translation of the Latin one
in Calvin's *Commentarii*, p. 54. See also Pareus, p. 69; Udall, sig. K2ᵛ; Perkins,
pp. 138-39; Manton, pp. 186-87.

Verum nec tunc quidem necessitate coactus esuriit, qui praeest
naturae, sed voluntate. . . . Aderat enim Christo facultas seipsum
absque cibo servandi: sed concessit quando voluit humanae naturae
quae sua sunt pati et agere; [29]

but Fuller writes that " God . . . who had formerly tied up his
appetite, now let it loose again," and Manton that " Gods
Providence permitted it, that he might be more capable of
Satans temptations." [30] Furthermore, though the mass of theologians were willing to concede that Christ went into the wilderness knowing that the temptation would follow, Pareus is even
prepared to deny that he foresaw it at all: " Ipse Dominus
haud dubie hunc finem non intendebat." [31]

Such differences of opinion, however, were evidently considered matters of minor importance, for they provoked no
actual controversy except when commentators went so far as
to suggest that Satan must have attacked Christ as he did
ordinary human beings—by putting evil thoughts into his mind.
Udall, for example, argues:

How can his temptations be our comfort when wee are tempted,
if they were of divers kinds? For it is evident, that the temptations
of Gods children be inward by cogitations, and therefore the holy
ghost in the Epistle to the Hebrewes, sayth notably, that he was
tempted in all thinges like unto us, this onely excepted: that his
temptations were in him without sinne.[32]

This hypothesis received some support from the argument that
Satan must have transported Christ to the temple and the high
mountain by means of visions, since the temptation is supposed
to have taken place in the desert,[33] and the kingdoms are shown
only in a moment of time.[34] Thomas Aquinas, however, dis-
misses the first reason because the trial is not said to have taken

---

[29] Luca, col. 531. See also St. Hilary, *Commentarius in Matthaeum*, cols. 928-29;
Theophylactus, *Enarratio in Evangelium Matthaei*, col. 179; Diodate (sec. sig.
C3^r): " that divine power gave way to let his humane nature voluntarily feel want
and discommodity."
[30] Fuller, p. 29; Manton, p. 30. See also Pareus (p. 65): " Hauddubie [esuriit]
nō tantum spōte, sed etiam necessitate naturae, ut se verū hominem declararet."
[31] Pareus, p. 64. For a full discussion of the whole point, see below, Chapter III,
pp. 30-31.
[32] Udall, sig. C7^v. See also J. Taylor, p. 143.
[33] St. Thomas Aquinas, *Summa Theologica*, pars 3, quaest. 41, art. 2. See also
Bucer, fol. 98.
[34] Bilson, p. 308.

place exclusively in the desert, and Bilson the second because the word "moment" may mean simply a "short period": "the deuill took no long time to shew those things, and Christ took lesse to beholde them; . . . I verily thinke he would not vouchsafe all earthly pompe any longer view than the turning of an eye to it, and from it." But the chief objection to either temptation-by-vision or temptation-by-thought sprang from the belief that the devil had no power over Christ's mind and imagination, because both were much too pure to be susceptible of such corruption, as ours are. The best he could do, therefore, was to make direct suggestions, from without — "foris, non intus."[35] So the great majority of commentators were content to suggest merely that Satan took the Lord to the temple or mountain on foot, or carried him there through the air (the more popular theory),[36] while their opinion of the temptation-by-thought hypothesis is best expressed by Diodate:

And therefore let confusion stop the mouthes of those blasphemous wretches, who pretending to new Lights, and extraordinary Illuminations, belch out this damnable Heresie, That when Christ was tempted, he was tempted by his own Corruption: when it is evident, that the Devil *had nothing in him*, as himself professeth *John* 14. 30 and therefore could not tempt him any way but Externally, and the *medium* of sense, by speaking to him, and presenting visible objects to his sight.[37]

Still, the very fact that such a view could be seriously suggested and find followers is perhaps some proof of how deeply commentators' thoughts of the temptation were colored by the belief that Christ undertook it as a human being.

It is in the light of all this accumulated tradition—and the acceptance of it implied in *The Christian Doctrine*—that we must, I think, consider the fact that the Christ of *Paradise*

[35] See for example: Bede, *In Matthaei Evangelium Expositio*, col. 19; St. Gregory the Great, col. 1135; Rabanus Maurus, *In Matthaeum*, col. 781; T. Taylor, p. 74; Piscator, p. 48; Ward, p. 87; Mayer, p. 77; Maldonatus, col. 89; Lapide, p. 101; Blackwood, p. 93; Manton, pp. 31-33; Chemnitius, p. 41; Balthasar Cordier, *Symbolarum in Matthaeum Tomas Prior [-Alter]*, (Tolosae, 1646-47), p. 49.

[36] Euthymius Zigabenus (col. 178) and Maldonatus (col. 89) favor the first method of transportation, but Lapide (p. 103) rejects it because the distances involved were too great. The second method is chosen by Lapide (p. 103), Blackwood (p. 96), Fuller (p. 72), Manton (p. 55), Woodhead (p. 117), etc.

[37] Diodate, sec. sig. A3ʳ. See also Bilson, p. 305; Woodhead, p. 117; Knox, pp. 106-7; T. Taylor, p. 74.

Regained is treated primarily and almost exclusively as "the
utmost of meer man both wise and good, / Not more,"[38] to
use the words in which Satan sums up all he knows of his
victim's character at the beginning of the third temptation.
From the very first, it is Christ's humanity which Milton em-
phasizes and insists on: "one mans firm obedience fully tri'd";
"th'exalted man, to whom / Such high attest was giv'n";
"this man of men, attested Son of God."[39] Even the Father
speaks of him as a human creature rather than the filial deity:

> He now shall know I can produce a man
> Of female Seed, far abler to resist
> All his sollicitations, and at length
> All his vast force, and drive him back to Hell,
> Winning by Conquest what the first man lost
> By fallacy surpriz'd. But first I mean
> To exercise him in the Wilderness . . .
> His weakness shall o'recome Satanic strength
> And all the world, and mass of sinful flesh;
> That all the Angels and Ætherial Powesr,
> They now, and men hereafter may discern,
> From what consummate vertue I have chose
> This perfect Man, by merit call'd my Son,
> To earn Salvation for the Sons of men.[40]

And it is very much "this perfect Man" that we see in the
wilderness: uncertain why he has been led there;[41] trying to
determine what he is to think of the hunger which has suddenly come upon him by no will of his own, but because God
permits it and "Nature hath need of what she asks"; wondering, "Where will this end?"; and meeting the devil's attacks
with a wisdom, rectitude, and piety so completely human that
Satan is finally compelled to use violence in order to discover

> what more thou art then man,
> Worth naming Son of God by voice from Heav'n.[42]

Taken by and in itself, such preoccupation with the lower
aspect of Christ's dual nature may well raise the question
whether, by the time he wrote *Paradise Regained*, Milton still
believed in the Lord's divinity at all. We know that when he

---

[38] *P. R.*, 4. 535-36.   [39] *P. R.*, 1. 4; 1. 36-37; 1. 122.   [40] *P. R.*, 1. 150-67.
[41] This and the following references are from *P. R.*, 1. 290-93; 2. 245-59; 2. 244.
[42] *P. R.*, 4. 538-39.

composed *The Christian Doctrine*, he was an Arian: is it not at least possible that his faith in the Trinity deteriorated still further as the years went on? Even though unacquainted with *The Christian Doctrine*, the very able and acute Calton was complaining as early as 1751 that in the Father's address to the angels, "not a word is said of the Son of God, but what a Socinian would allow." [43] Something of the same suspicion seems to lie behind Tillyard's more recent contention that

Christ is no longer in the main the Redeemer of man. He merely typifies the way in which the human soul can be regencrated. The Pauline fabric of fall, grace, redemption, and regeneration, seems to have crumbled.[44]

W. G. Rice, too, asserts that "[Milton] is getting behind the accretions of theological speculation and dogma, and figuring forth the Christ of the New Testament, the Greater Man"; [45] and Denis Saurat had apparently reached a similar conclusion when he argued that in his final period, Milton lost even the last remnants of his belief in the doctrine of the Trinity: "the Christ-Son of God . . . as Jesus, fades more and more into mere man." [46]

All such theories, however, are open to the objection that they cannot, in the nature of the case, be proved—at least, not by internal evidence found in *Paradise Regained*. We cannot be sure that Milton was deliberately trying to "get behind" the accretions of speculation and dogma; for all we know, he may have been basing his work directly on those speculations, many authors of which emphasize the humanity of Christ almost as much as he does. Nor can we be certain that he has given up the Pauline fabric of fall, grace, redemption, and regeneration; according to orthodox opinion, it was simply *by* typifying the way in which the human soul can be regenerated that Christ carried out his redemptive function within that fabric during the temptation. Nor does the fact that Christ tends to fade into "mere man" necessarily mean that Milton

---

[43] Calton, note on 1. 163 of *Paradise Regained*, ed. Thomas Newton, "with notes of Various Authors" (London, 1785), 1. 16.

[44] E. M. W. Tillyard, *Milton* (London, 1930), p. 305.

[45] W. G. Rice, "*Paradise Regained*," *Papers of the Michigan Academy of Sciences, Arts, and Letters* 22. 496.

[46] Denis Saurat, *Milton: Man and Thinker* (New York, 1925), pp. 238-39.

was any more of an anti-Trinitarian when he wrote *Paradise Regained* than he was when he wrote *Paradise Lost* or *The Christian Doctrine*: he may merely have been complying with his own theory that the temptation was one of the occasions on which Christ was " affected chiefly and most visibly in his human nature." And we have some evidence which suggests that this was actually the case.

In the first place, Milton stops short of the logical extremity to which the belief that Christ was tempted as a man had carried some Renaissance commentators: he does not imply that Christ was tempted inwardly, "by his own Corruption." He hews instead to the conventional line that the devil attacked the Lord only "Externally . . . by speaking to him, and presenting visible objects to his sight." Satan is once allowed to disturb his victim with "ugly dreams," [47] but he is granted no power over the mind of Christ when it is awake and on guard. We may argue, of course, that Milton had no real objection to making the temptation *intus, non foris*, but simply found it easier to present it as an external rather than an internal one. Still, the difficulties of formulating the trial in subjective terms were not insurmountable; and the fact that he did not do so is interesting, though not conclusive.

We should also note that while Milton went further than the majority in refusing Christ foreknowledge of the temptation or power over his own appetite, he does little more than conform to a trend already present in Protestant theology, and emphasize points already made by other scholars, for very good reasons. Even a convinced Arian might, without denying his principles, have given the Lord either privilege, if he had taken care to point out that both foreknowledge and power were bestowed on him by the Spirit. But to do so would be to deny him that uncertainty about the future and that inability to control the present which form no inconsiderable part of the ordinary man's tribulations, and incline him most to listen to the persuasions and promises of Satan. Milton's treatment of the subject is more satisfactory. It not only avoids any suggestion that Christ suffered less than we do, but enables the poet to bring out to the full his perfect trust and confidence in the Father:

[47] *P. R.*, 4. 408.

> And now by some strong motion I am led
> Into this Wilderness, to what intent
> I learn not yet; perhaps I need not know;
> For what concerns my knowledge God reveals.[48]

And again:

> [I] from the sting of famine fear no harm,
> Nor mind it, fed with better thoughts that feed
> Mee hungring more to do my Fathers will.[49]

Finally, at the conclusion of the struggle — the time which the tradition reserved for the open acknowledgment of Christ's divinity — the angels appear and acclaim him in no uncertain terms as the filial deity, identical with the Son of *Paradise Lost*:

> True Image of the Father whether thron'd
> In the bosom of bliss, and light of light
> Conceiving, or remote from Heaven, enshrin'd
> In fleshly Tabernacle, and human form,
> Wandring the Wilderness, whatever place,
> Habit or state, or motion, still expressing
> The Son of God, with Godlike force indu'd
> Against th'Attempter of thy Fathers Throne,
> And Thief of Paradise; him long of old
> Thou didst debel, and down from Heav'n cast
> With all his Army, now thou hast aveng'd
> Supplanted *Adam*, and by vanquishing
> Temptation, hast regained lost Paradise,
> And frustrated the conquest fraudulent.[50]

This demonstration is all the more remarkable in view of the fact that Milton had, ready to his hand, another conventional elucidation of the text which he could have used without committing himself to open support of Christ's divinity. He might have made the song of the angels simply a proclamation that as they ministered to Christ, so they would minister to any other human being who had fought and overcome the devil. But significantly enough, Milton did not choose to do so.

It follows, I think, that we have no reason to assume that in 1671 Milton's basic conception of the nature and function of the Redeemer did not remain exactly what it had been in 1667. Furthermore, it is handled very much as it had been in 1667. C. S. Lewis has reminded us that Milton does not go out of his

---

[48] *P. R.*, 1. 290-93.   [49] *P. R.*, 2. 257-59.   [50] *P. R.*, 596-609.

way to parade his heresies in *Paradise Lost*: that they rarely appear in the poem itself, and when they do, are presented in so ambiguous a form that it is difficult to detect them without the aid of external evidence from *The Christian Doctrine* or what we know of Milton's private reading.[51] This is equally true of *Paradise Regained*. Nothing in the work actually contradicts the Arian opinions expressed in *The Christian Doctrine*: it may even be those opinions which make the poet dwell a little too emphatically on the superiority of the Father and the dutiful subordination of the Son. But since no one denied that the Son *quasi homo* was necessarily inferior and subordinate to the Father, and since it is the Son *quasi homo* who dominates *Paradise Regained*, an instructed seventeenth-century reader would not find the presentation of Christ unorthodox and perhaps not even surprising. In essentials, it is entirely consistent with the established view of Milton's day, which Robert Hill ably sums up as: "Fasting and an hungry, to shew he was man: fighting and encountering, to shew he was Messiah; and conquering and triumphing, to shew he was God."[52] And since Milton must have known how his work would appear to his audience, we can only conclude that he was satisfied that it should be so.

---

[51] C. S. Lewis, *A Preface to Paradise Lost* (London, 1943), pp. 85-89.
[52] Robert Hill, *Epistle Dedicatorie* to Perkins' *Satans Sophistrie*, sig. A2ᵛ.

CHAPTER III

MOTIVATION: GOD, CHRIST, AND SATAN

Throughout the Middle Ages and the Renaissance all orthodox theologians assumed that the unspecified "spirit" which
led Christ to the scene of the temptation was the Holy Ghost
which had just descended on him at the baptism, and of which
he was said to be "full" when he returned from Jordan.[1] This
was taken to mean that the temptation was not entirely the
work of the devil, but an event instituted and permitted by
God. It was easy to see why. In the first place, the temptation
was an essential part of the whole scheme of redemption,
whereby Christ restored

the work of God to his original perfection. In the bringing of which
to pass it was decreed by God in the beginning as a thing necessary, that the head of the serpent, by whose means it was violated
and defaced, should be bruised. And "for this cause," saith Saint
John, "appeared the Son of God, that He might loose the works
of the devil," whereof this was the first. For in Genesis, the third
chapter, we read that his first work after his fall was enviously to
tempt our first parents, and thereby to overthrow all mankind. . . .
Christ therefore first beginneth with the overcoming of that; and

---

[1] See for example: Bede, *In Lucae Evangelium Expositio, Patr. Lat.* 92. col. 366;
St. Ambrose, *Expositionis in Lucam*, col. 1701; St. Hilary, *Commentarius in Mat-
thaeum*, col. 928; St. Jerome, col. 31; Cajetanus, *In S. Marcum Commentaria* [1530],
Script. Sacr. Cursus Compl. 22. col. 25; Calvin, *Commentarii*, p. 51; Knox, 4. 99;
Henry Hammond, *A Paraphrase and Annotations upon All the Books of the New
Testament* (London, 1671), p. 19; Perkins, p. 7; Mayer, p. 77; Maldonatus, col. 85;
Lapide, p. 98; Chemnitius, p. 36; Blackwood, p. 89; Manton, p. 3; Cradock, p. 39;
Joseph Hall, *A Plaine and Familiar Explication of all the Hard Texts of the Old
and New Testament* (London, 1633), p. 6; etc. Apparently, however, there was
some feeling that the "spirit" might be the devil, for both Bede and Knox go out
of their way to insist that it was not. St. Bruno Astensius (cols. 90-91) thought
that even if Christ had been led into the desert by Satan

non esset inconveniens, cum Lucas Evangelistas eum in Jerusalem et in montem
excelsum valde a diabolo non assumptum, sed ductum apertissime dicat. Quod
si ibi, et ibi ab alio spiritu ductum esse non est inconveniens; quare in desertum
quoque ab alio spiritu eum ductum fuisse inconveniens videatur?

But he admits that all orthodox opinion favored the view that the guide was the
Holy Spirit, and does not reject it.

for that purpose He is here led forth to be tempted, that so being tempted he might overcome.[2]

Again, it was necessary that Christ, as man, should prove his worth by actual conflict with Satan: "for an exercise of his humiliation, and a triall of his perfect holiness and righteousness, and of his victory over the Devil by the power thereof. And to give his Church a proof of assured victory against all the endeavors and subtleties of the evil spirit."[3] Furthermore, it was fitting that Christ, as Head of the Church, should undergo temptation in order to show his followers how they could best overcome it.[4] Finally, and rather touchingly, the trial is said to have been planned by heaven "that our Lord might the better know how to pitty, and tender, and relieue us with comforts, when we are in temptation."[5]

Like the great mass of theologians, Milton believed that Christ was guided by the Holy Ghost, as is immediately evident from the prayer with which the poem opens:

> Thou Spirit who led'st this glorious Eremite
> Into the Desert, his Victorious Field
> Against the Spiritual Foe, and brought'st him thence
> By proof the undoubted Son of God, inspire
> As thou art wont, my prompted song else mute.[6]

He also assigns two of the four conventional motives to God the Father, Who tells Gabriel at the council in heaven:

---

[2] Andrewes, pp. 479-80. See also St. Paschasius Radbertus, *Expositio in Matthaeum, Patr. Lat.* 120. cols 186-87; Pareus, p. 64; Baxter, p. 5; Dyke, p. 222; Ward, pp. 86-87; Perkins, p. 9; Capel, p. 100; Cradock, p. 39; Woodhead, p. 112; Chemnitius, p. 36.

[3] Diodate, sec. sig. C3ʳ. See also, Lapide, pp. 98-99; Hammond, p. 19; Johannes Clericus, *Harmonia Evangelica cui Subjuncta est Historia Jesu Christi* (London, 1700), p. 18; Cassiodorus, cols. 983-84; Pareus, p. 64; St. Hilary, *Tractatus in CXXXVIII Psalmum*, col. 794-96.

[4] St. Paschasius Radbertus, cols. 186-87; Luca, cols. 527-29; Pareus, p. 64; Piscator, p. 57; Ward, p. 87; Perkins, p. 19; Mayer, p. 77; Lapide, pp. 98-99; Chemnitius, p. 36; Blackwood, pp. 89-90; Woodhead, p. 112; St. Thomas Aquinas, *Summa Theologica*, pars 3; quaest. 41, art. 1. St. Thomas adds that the temptation is designed to show us that no one should think he is so holy that he can avoid such trials.

[5] Dyke, p. 222. See also Ward, p. 86; Perkins, pp. 19-20; Blackwood, p. 89; Fuller, p. 13; Woodhead, p. 112. See also St. Thomas Aquinas (*Summa Theologica*, pars 3, quaest. 41, art. 1): "ut nobis fiduciam de sua misericordia largiretur."

[6] *P. R.*, 1.8-12.

> this day *by proof* thou shalt behold,
> Thou and all Angels conversant on Earth
> With man or men's affairs, how I begin
> To verify that solemn message late,
> On which I sent thee to the Virgin pure
> In Galilee, that she should bear a Son
> Great in Renown, and call'd the Son of God . . .
> this man born and now up-grown
> *To show him worthy of his birth divine*
> *And high prediction, henceforth I expose*
> *To Satan* . . .
> He now shall know I can produce a man
> Of female Seed, far abler to resist
> All his solicitations, and at length
> All his vast force, and drive him back to Hell,
> *Winning by Conquest what the first man lost*
> By fallacy surpris'd. But first I mean
> To *exercise* him in the Wilderness;
> *There he shall first lay down the rudiments*
> *Of his great warfare,* ere I send him forth
> To conquer Sin and Death the two grand foes,
> By Humiliation and strong Sufferance:
> His weakness shall o'ercome Satanic strength
> And all the world, and mass of sinful flesh;
> That all the Angels and Æthereal Powers,
> They now, and men hereafter, may discern
> From what consummate virtue I have chose
> This perfect Man, *by merit* call'd my Son,
> *To earn Salvation for the Sons of men.*[7]

Unlike his predecessors, however, Milton does not emphasize the exemplary function of the temptation, for when God says that men are to "discern" Christ's virtue, He apparently means no more than that they are to recognize and acknowledge it. As in *Paradise Lost*, he presents his work as a narrative of the facts, and avoids the *argumentum ad hominem* proper to a tract or a homily. Nowhere in the poem does he suggest openly that the Lord is laying down a law for the tempted, or even that Christians under similar circumstances would do well to follow his example. The moral lesson of *Paradise Regained* may be obvious, but every reader is left to draw it for himself. It is less easy to understand (or excuse) his omission of the hypothesis that Christ was to learn to "pitty and tender us." Perhaps he felt that it too belonged in a sermon rather than in a poem;

[7] *P. R.,* 1. 130-67, *passim.* Italics mine.

perhaps he thought it out of place in the militant address of God the Father; or perhaps its sweetness simply did not appeal to his own austere and fastidious taste.

The majority of exegetes assumed that Christ went into the wilderness fully aware of what was to follow, and determined to endure it for the same reasons that his Father chose to inflict it: to redeem mankind,[8] to prove his worth,[9] to set an example to his followers,[10] and to learn how to sympathize with them most fully.[11] Apparently, even those commentators who present the motives of God without assigning any to Christ do so merely to avoid repetition, since they never say outright that he did not know there was to be a temptation. In addition, he was frequently credited with a desire to prepare himself for his mission by prayer and fasting: "Per istud tempus haud dubie meditatus est Christus prophetias Evangelicas per ipsum implendas: ut hac quoque ratione praepararetur ad muneris sui functionem."[12] Therefore, when Pareus decided that the Lord had better not have foreknowledge of the temptation, it was easy for him to assert that Christ went into the desert simply to arm himself for the future:

Ipse Dominus haud dubie hunc finem non intendebat: sed potius ut jejunio et precibus ibi se muneri accingeret: Spiritus vero aliud spectabat, ut occasione solitudinis et jejunii tentaretur.[13]

Milton, for reasons which we have already discussed, takes much the same attitude that Pareus does. When his Christ goes into the wilderness, he knows that he is the promised Messiah, whose

> way must lie
> Through many a hard assay even to the death,
> Ere I the promis'd Kingdom can attain,

---

[8] St. Ambrose, *Expositionis in Lucam*, cols. 1697-1700; Bede, *In Lucae Evangelium Expositio*, col. 368; St. Leo the Great, col. 278; Jansen, col. 527; T. Taylor, pp. 35-36; Musculus, p. 43; Udall, sig. B4ᵛ–B5ʳ; Maldonatus, col. 85; Manton, pp. 11-12.

[9] Marlorate, p. 57; Calvin, *Commentarii*, p. 50; Manton, p. 15.

[10] St. Augustine, *Sermo CXXIII*, *Patr. Lat.* 38. col. 685; St. Bruno Astensius, cols. 92-93; St. Ambrose, *Expositionis in Lucam*, col. 1700; Chrysostom, cols. 207-9; Jansen, col. 528; Musculus, p. 45; T. Taylor, p. 26; Udall, sig. B5ʳ; Bucer, fol. 98; Manton, p. 17.

[11] Maldonatus, col. 85; Manton, p. 13.

[12] Piscator, p. 48. See also Maldonatus, col. 85; Luca, cols. 530-31; B. Aretius, *Commentarii in Evangelium Secundum Marcum* (Lansanne, 1579), p. 39.

[13] Pareus, p. 64.

> Or work Redemption for mankind, whose sins
> Full weight must be transferr'd upon my head; [14]

and he passes his time there meditating on his plans for his ministry:

> with such thoughts
> Accompanied of things past and to come
> Lodg'd in his breast, as well 'might recommend
> Such Solitude before choicest Society . . . [15]
> All his great work to come before him set;
> How to begin, how to accomplish best
> His end of being on Earth, and mission high. [16]

But while he realizes that he has a redemptive function to perform, and is entirely willing to carry it out in any manner God sees fit, he is not aware that he has been brought to the desert to begin it:

> And now by some strong motion I am led
> Into this Wilderness, to what intent
> I learn not yet; perhaps I need not know;
> For what concerns my knowledge God reveals. [17]

The motives which led Satan to undertake the temptation were a matter of dispute. During both the Middle Ages and Renaissance, it was widely assumed that his chief object in attempting to seduce Christ was to find out if he really were the Son of God. The perfection of the Lord's character, his miraculous birth, and the acknowledgment from Heaven which he had received at his baptism, had already warned the devil that the promised Messiah was at hand; but when he saw that Messiah hungering in the wilderness, he began to doubt his identity, because his own pride was so great that he could not bring himself to believe that any divine personage would submit to suffering like a mere human being. Confused but suspicious, he turned to the temptation as a means of settling the question. As Bede puts it:

Qui tamen prius cum hunc passibilem cerneret, cum posse mortalia perpeti humanitatis videret, omne quod de ejus divinitate suspicatus est, ei fastu suae superbiae in in dubium venit. Nihil quippe,

---

[14] *P. R.*, 1. 263-67.
[15] *P. R.*, 1. 300-4.
[16] *P. R.*, 2. 112-14.
[17] *P. R.*, 1. 290-93.

nisi superbum sapiens, dum esse hunc humilem conspicit, Deum esse dubitabit. Unde ad tentationem se argumenta convertit.[18]

Leigh, on the other hand, writes as if Satan were chiefly bewildered by the fact that he could not determine whether the proclamation that Christ was the Son of God meant that he was "the Son of God by nature, or onely his adopted Son by grace":

Perceiving that this man was called the Son of God by the Father and *Iohn* the Baptist, he would try whether He was the true Son of God; that he might poure out upon him his ancient envy, anger, and indignation. Therefore it is probable (saith à Lapide) that the Devill did not at first abruptly say to him, *If thou beest the Son of God*, but that he first courteously saluted him, and by faire speeches insinuated himselfe into him, saying, what my Lord dost thou here alone, what dost thou muse on? I saw thee baptised in Jordane, and heard a voyce from heaven saying, this is my Son, I desire to know whether thou beest truely the Son of God by nature, or only his adopted Son by grace. I see also that by fasting forty dayes thou art very hungry, therefore if thou beest the Son of God satisfie thy hunger, and turne those stones to bread; for it will be very easie for thee to do it.[19]

Satan's suggestions, then, are subtly contrived not only to corrupt Christ's virtue, but to elicit from him some acknowledgment of his divinity. "It seemeth," Diodate writes,

the Devill had two ends in these temptations, the one to draw from Christ some proofs or trials of his Deity, and of the mystery of his Incarnation, of which he had but an obscure knowledge: which was denied him, as miracles were to unbelievers and profane men. The other was to draw his humane nature to sin.[20]

Therefore, as St. Ambrose observes, the first temptation begins with the phrase, "If thou art the Son of God":

---

[18] Bede, *In Lucae Evangelium Expositio*, col. 367. See also St. Hilary, *Commentarius in Matthaeum*, col. 928; J. Wyclif, *Sermons on the Gospels*, in *Select Works*, ed. T. Arnold (Oxford, 1869), 1.109; Ludolphus of Saxony, *Vie de Jesus-Christ* [fifteenth century], trans. by A. L. de La Marche (Paris, 1870), pp. 77-78; *Ludus Coventriae*, p. 194; St. Thomas Aquinas, *Summa Theologica*, pars 3, quaest. 41, art. 1; Musculus, pp. 47-49; Jansen, cols. 531-33; Beza, p. 12; Mayer, p. 78; More, p. 7; Cordier, p. 47; Lapide, p. 102; Woodhead, p. 113; Chemnitius, p. 41.

[19] Leigh, p. 104. See also Lapide, p. 102; Maldonatus, col. 87; and Blackwood, p. 93; Euthymius Zigabenus, cols. 174-75.

[20] Diodate, sec. sig. C3ʳ.

Sed quid sibi vult talis sermonis exorsus: *Si Filius Dei es*; nisi quia cognoverat Dei Filium esse venturum? Sed venisse per hance infirmitatem corporis non putebat. Aliud explorantis, aliud tentantis est; et Deo se profitetur credere, et homini conatur illudere.[21]

In other words, if Christ failed to turn the stones into bread, or denied his ability to do so, he would be proved no Messiah, and hence no danger to Satan. If, however, he succeeded in turning the stones into bread, he would be proved the Messiah, but still no danger to Satan, since the very act which reveals his power ruins the Second Adam as effectively as the First, "Satan knowing he could not save others, who sinned himself."[22] St. Jerome, rather less logically, argues that if the devil once discovered that Christ was really the Son of God, he would realize that it was useless to tempt him.[23] This, of course, would be disastrous, since the success of the whole plan of redemption depended upon Christ's meeting and overcoming all three attacks.[24]

The temptation of the tower is another suggestion of the same order. The temptation of the kingdoms, however, fell into a slightly different category, since it did not entail any display of the Lord's divine power, or include the familiar opening: *Si Filius Dei es*. Luca, however, argues that Satan's impudent assertion that he owned the world was intended to provoke some counter-claim from Christ.[25] I. H., on the other hand, contends that after the temptation of the tower, "the diuel, seeing that he could not perceaue nothing of his deity, & supposing thereby that he was not God, but a meere man, he began the third time to tempt him as he was man."[26] The authors of the *Assembly's Annotations* present still a third theory: "hence it appears why Satan begins not as before; If thou be the Son of God: for he knew that Christ if he took

[21] St. Ambrose, *Expositionis in Lucam*, col. 1701. See also Chrysostom, cols. 210-11; St. Hilary, *Commentarius in Matthaeum*, col. 929; St. Jerome, col. 32; Udall, sig. C8ʳ; Ward, p. 96; Perkins, p. 36; More, p. 7; Maldonatus, col. 84; Lapide, p. 102; Blackwood, p. 93; Fuller, pp. 10-12; Chemnitius, p. 42.

[22] Fuller, p. 10. See also Maldonatus, col. 84.

[23] St. Jerome, col. 32.

[24] See Chapter V.

[25] Luca, cols. 537-38. See also Jansen, cols. 536-37; Lapide, p. 107; Woodhead, p. 119.

[26] I. H., *The Life of our Lord and Saviour Jesus Christ* (N. p., 1634), p. 273.

himself to be the Son of God, would not worship him: and if
he were not so, he might peradventure be willing to accept of
Satan's large offer."[27] Christopher Blackwood (a cautious
spirit) gives all three explanations in order, without attempting
to judge of their merits.[28]

From the hypothesis that Satan undertook the temptation
to learn whether Christ was the Messiah, some writers went on
to draw the conclusion that Christ's answers were deliberately
designed to conceal the secret of his own identity. He refuses
to sin, but in doing so neither denies nor affirms his divinity,
because he is equally unwilling to tell a flat lie, or to give his
opponent the satisfaction of finding what he has come to seek.[29]
Hence, at the end of the temptation, Satan leaves the wilderness
still more uncertain of Christ's real nature than he was when
he came:

> Out out harrow Alas Alas
> I wondyr sore what is he this
> I can not brynge hym to no trespas
> nere be no synne to don a-mys
> he byddyth me gon a-bakke
> What þat he is I kan not se
> Whethyr god or man what þat he be
> I kan not telle in no degre
> For sorwe I lete a crakke.[30]

Since, however, the Evangelists afterwards state that the
devils recognized Christ when he cast them out of the sick,
Fuller preferred to argue that Satan *had* discovered Christ's
identity by the end of the temptation:

He (who so long had look'd for that which he was loath to finde,
viz. whether Christ was the Son of God) was now [when Christ
told him to depart] to his great sorrow, sufficiently satisfied in the
affirmative, that he was so; and therefore desisted from farther
inquiry therein.

---

[27] *Assembly Annotations*, sig. A4ᵛ. See also Maldonatus, col. 84, and Fuller,
p. 148.

[28] Blackwood, pp. 104-5.

[29] Ludolphus of Saxony, p. 78; *Ludus Coventriae*, p. 199; Luca, col. 545; Jansen,
col. 546; Perkins, p. 14; Maldonatus, col. 88; I. H., p. 270; Blackwood, p. 95; Pseudo-
Bonaventura, *Meditations on the Life of Christ*, trans. Sister Mary Emmanuel (Saint
Louis, 1934), pp. 107-8.

[30] *Ludus Coventriae*, p. 199. See also Jansen, col. 546; Luca, col. 545; Lapide,
pp. 104-5; Aelfric, 1. 177.

It is observable, how much Satans knowledge was (I will not say bettered, but) increased in one Chapter (Mark 1) within the compass of eleven verses. For, verse 13. he *tempted* Christ, namely, to try *whether he was the Son of God*; and verse 24. *he confesseth him: I knowe thee* (with deare-bought knowledge, to his owne confusion) *who thou art, the holy One of God.*[31]

Woodhead, more carefully, writes not that Satan was "satisfied" and "desisted," but that he knew Christ to be divine when he found himself unable to disobey the command to leave him. "By the power of which words," he adds, "our Lord at last manifested that which he was not pleased to shew at Satans request."[32] In other words, as Woodhead implies, his hypothesis has the advantage of preserving the best feature of the alternative theory: that Christ saw through and frustrated the clever devices by which the devil attempted to win the secret from him. It should also be noted that in the Old English *Christ and Satan*, Jesus lays his commands on the tempter "by most high might," and tells him that "thou hast met the Maker of creation, the Lord of man,"[33] as he compels him to return to hell. Since *Christ and Satan* includes only the temptation of the kingdoms, we cannot determine whether the writer thought that Satan doubted the Lord's identity until he finally learned the truth in this particular manner, but the placing and wording of the lines suggest that he did. The great majority of exegetes, however, arrive at no conclusion of any kind: they merely state that the devil tried to discover if Christ was the Messiah, and then drop the whole question, without troubling to inform their readers whether he succeeded or not.[34]

During the Renaissance, on the other hand, we find a certain number of Protestant theologians rejecting the hypothesis *in toto*, and asserting that Satan had no doubt that Christ was the promised Messiah. They argue either that the devil was making a desperate effort to subvert him before he could begin

---

[31] Fuller, p. 177.

[32] Woodhead, p. 120. See also St. Hilary, *Commentarius in Matthaeum*, cols. 930-31: "Temeritatis tantae congruum exitum tulit, cum et criminum suorum in *satana* nomen audivit, et Dominum Deum suum adorandum in homine cognovit."

[33] *The Caedmon Poems*, trans., Charles W. Kennedy (London, 1916), p. 172.

[34] See for example: Bede, *In Matthaei Evangelium Expositio*, col. 20; Wyclif, p. 112; Beza, p. 12; Musculus, p. 53; etc.

his work,[35] or, " as an angry dog bites a stone out of meer mad-
ness, though knowing that he shall sooner break his teeth, then
batter the stone: so Satans malice so far transported and
blinded his judgment, that he tempted Christ, though (knowing him for the Son of God) his temptations would prove
ineffectual." [36] It followed that the devil did not use the phrase,
Si Filius Dei es, because he was uncertain of the Lord's divinity
or hoped to provoke some admission of it, but merely because
he meant to shake Christ's faith in his own powers, and to
" impugne God's word and oracle from heaven." [37]

Milton, however, was evidently unconvinced by such arguments or of the opinion that the introduction of the doubt
motif would make for a better-knit and more exciting story.
His devil does not know whether Christ is the promised Messiah
or not, though " his birth to our just fear gave no small cause," [38]
and the perfection of his character " multiplies my fear." [39] But
he does not begin to have serious doubts of his identity only
when he sees him starving in the wilderness like any other
human being. Like Leigh's Satan, he is confused principally
because he feels that the testimony which the Lord has received
from heaven at his baptism has been ambiguous: that the term
" Son of God "

bears no single sense;
The Son of God I also am, or was,
And if I was, I am; relation stands;
All men are Sons of God.[40]

Therefore, though the miracle at the baptism convinces him
that Christ is indeed *a* Son of God, he is by no means sure that
he is *the* Son of God who is destined to conquer him:

> His first-begot we know, and sore have felt,
> When his fierce thunder drove us to the deep;
> Who this is we must learn, for man he seems
> In all his lineaments, though in his face
> The glimpses of his father's glory shine.[41]

---

[35] Marlorate, p. 57.
[36] Fuller, p. 40; he cites the theory as a possible alternative to his own. For other
instances, see Calvin, *Commentarii*, p. 50; Knox, 4. 108-9; T. Taylor, pp. 76-79;
Dyke, pp. 213 and 221; Trapp, p. 52; Downame, p. 2; Andrewes, pp. 487-88.
[37] T. Taylor, p. 79.
[38] *P. R.*, 1. 66.
[39] *P. R.*, 1. 69.
[40] *P. R.*, 1. 517-20.
[41] *P. R.*, 1. 89-93.

And so, when he goes to the wilderness, it is not only "to subvert" but to "subvert whom he suspected rais'd / To end his Reign on Earth so long enjoy'd," [42] and by subverting, "to understand my Adversary, who / And what he is." [43] His first approach to Christ is remarkably like that described as the proper one by Leigh and his fellow-commentators when they are discussing the question of Satan's motives: the same solicitous courtesy, the same reference to his presence at the baptism, the same "faire speeches" that gradually lead up to the real point.[44] Milton's handling of the scene, however, is much more subtle than theirs—the devil dwells longer on Christ's solitude and helplessness, and he suggests that the stones be turned to bread as an act of necessity and charity rather than a proof of the Lord's divinity. The doubt motif appears more openly at the temptation of the kingdoms, when Satan admits that

> I to try whether in higher sort
> Than [angels and men] thou bear'st that title, have propos'd
> What both from men and angels I receive,
> Tetrarchs of Fire, Air, Flood, and on the Earth
> Nations besides from all the quartered winds,
> God of this world invok'd and world beneath.[45]

The statement is vague, but sounds as if Milton were thinking of the theory that Satan hoped Christ would either prove himself less than divine by worshipping him, or would be provoked into making some counter-claim to the world which would set him above the men and angels who acknowledged Satan's right to it. Christ, in fact, does make a sort of counter-claim:

> Wert thou so void of fear and shame
> As offer them to me the Son of God,
> To me my own, on such abhorred pact? [46]

But the phrase "to me my own" is ambiguous: it may mean "the kingdoms you have offered me for my own," as well as "my own kingdoms." And in any event, Christ refuses to describe himself as anything but the Son of God, and not "the King of Kings, / God over all supreme," [47] who can give the

[42] P. R., 1. 124-25.
[43] P. R., 4. 527-28.
[44] Cf. above, pp. 57-58 and P. R., 1. 320-34.
[45] P. R., 4. 198-203.   [46] P. R., 4. 189-91.   [47] P. R., 4. 185-86.

earth to whom he chooses. This answer Satan finds completely
unsatisfactory, as he very carefully makes clear:

> Be not so sore offended, Son of God,
> Though Sons of God both angels are and men . . .
> The trial hath indamaged thee no way,
> Rather more honor left and more esteem;
> Me nought advantaged, missing what I aimed.[48]

The nature of the whole interchange here suggests strongly
that Milton's acceptance of the hypothesis that Satan undertook the temptation to determine the Lord's true identity had
entailed his acceptance of the secondary hypothesis that Christ
played his opponent along with veracious but evasive answers,
to prevent him from discovering the truth. The necessity for
such ambiguity on the Lord's part must have been one of the
matters which "concerned his knowledge," and which God, as
a result, "revealed." And that necessity may have affected
the poem far more deeply than a reader unfamiliar with the
tradition might suppose. It would do something, I think, to
explain why Christ meets all the devil's attacks as he does.
There were two possible ways of rejecting Satan's various
projects for his future: by exposing their worthlessness, or by
demonstrating the superiority of his own plans. For instance,
when the devil suggests that he spend his life seeking and
enjoying universal popular acclaim, he can reply effectively
either by proving that the masses are too vulgar and confused
to applaud the good, or by asserting that he intends to raise
them to the level where they will applaud the good. Again,
when Satan urges him to take over the Roman Empire in order
to rid a victor nation of a servile yoke, he can reply effectively
either by declaring that the Romans do not deserve their freedom, or by arguing that the liberty he will bestow on them is
greater than mere physical emancipation can be. The latter
defense seems so much more appropriate to the Saviour than
the former that it is the one we expect any writer with the least
feeling for Christianity to attribute to him. But in *Paradise
Regained*, this is not the case. Christ confines himself to pointing out the shoddiness of Satan's proposals or enumerating the
vices of the different groups he is called upon to lead. He may

[48] *P. R.*, 4. 196-208.

occasionally conclude an answer with a definition of true glory
or true leadership:

> But if there be in glory aught of good,
> It may by means far different be attain'd
> Without ambition, war or violence;
> By deeds of peace, by wisdom eminent,
> By patience, temperance; [49]

or again,

> But to guide Nations in the way of truth
> By saving Doctrine, and from errour lead
> To know, and knowing worship God aright,
> Is yet more Kingly, this attracts the Soul. [50]

Such passages, however, are curiously impersonal. Christ does
not say, "This is the sort of glory *I* shall seek," or, "This is
the manner in which *I* intend to rule." And the modern reader's
instinct is to resent what he conceives to be the distortion of
Christ's character by this union of so much reticence with so
much denunciation. While he does not actually wish the Lord
to entertain illusions about the ultimate worth of mob-applause
or physical freedom, he cannot see any reason why the severity
of Christ's strictures upon those illusions might not be balanced
and mitigated by fuller and more positive discussion of his own
sympathies and plans. Why should his projects for the future
be so largely defined by negatives? Why should he declare what
form the Kingdom is not to take, but not what form it is to
take, or in what way he proposes to reign over it? Why does
he inform Satan only that

> Means there shall be to this, but what the means,
> Is not for thee to know, or me to tell? [51]

But the phrase, "is not for thee to know," again suggests
that Milton was working under the influence of the tradition
that Christ deliberately withheld from Satan all evidence of
his own identity. The "means" by which the Lord proposed
to better mankind were part of that evidence. When we remember that to Milton and his audience the "Kingdom" was
not vaguely synonymous with "the good society," but stood
for fallen humanity restored by the incarnation and sacrifice

[49] *P. R.*, 3. 89-93.   [50] *P. R.*, 2. 473-76.   [51] *P. R.*, 4. 152-53.

of the divine, it is easy to understand why the poet may have felt that since the manner of the Saviour's reign was so inextricably bound up with the mystery of his real nature, Christ could not very well discuss the one without revealing the other. He is therefore obliged to rely almost entirely on the second possible line of defense—unqualified condemnation and rebuke. It was a line of defense so little in harmony with Christ's character as a whole that a writer more overwhelmingly conscious of the personality of Jesus might well have avoided it at any cost. Moreover, there is certainly some degree of coldness and insensitivity in Milton's failure to realize that under the circumstances, the condemnation of men's failings ought to be as gentle and compassionate as possible. The most we can do is argue that the nature of the tradition made it disastrously easy to slip into such faults, and may have prevented the introduction of material which might otherwise have softened and completed the presentation of the hero. But unattractive as Christ's handling of the situation may be, it accomplishes its purpose. At the beginning of the final day, Satan is still as uncertain of the Lord's real nature as he was at the beginning of the first.

Milton, however, had no intention of permitting the devil to go away unsatisfied and dubious, as he does in the *Ludus Coventriae*. As a writer, he would probably object to so lame and flat a resolution of the doubt motif: to bring the theme to a full and perfect conclusion within the poem, Satan obviously ought to be made aware of the Lord's true identity at the last, though not in any manner which he has foreseen, or which gratifies him in the least. As a theologian, too, Milton was doubtless familiar with the argument that the demons recognize and acknowledge Christ to be the Son of God after the temptation; and it is perhaps significant that the angels refer to one such episode in the song of triumph at the conclusion of the poem:

> Hereafter learn with awe
> To dread the Son of God: He all unarm'd
> Shall chase thee with the terror of his voice
> From thy demoniac holds, possession foul,
> Thee and thy legions, yelling they shall fly,

> And beg to hide them in a herd of swine,
> Lest he command them down into the Deep,
> Bound and to torment sent before their time.[52]

But Milton was not, apparently, prepared to follow the conventional hypothesis that the discovery came when Satan was compelled to depart after the temptation of the kingdoms. His efforts to find a different solution to the problem probably resulted from his peculiar and untraditional interpretation of the temptation of the tower.

---

[52] *P. R.*, 4. 625-32. Cf. Luke 8:28: " When [the lunatic in the country of the Gaderenes] saw Jesus, he cried out . . . ' What have I to do with thee, Jesus, thou Son of God most high? ' "

CHAPTER IV

THE DISGUISE ASSUMED BY SATAN

The hypothesis that Satan had assumed a disguise at the temptation rested on the supposition that he had appeared in the wilderness in a corporeal form. This in its turn rested on the argument that since he was powerless to attack Christ as he did ordinary human beings, all he could do was make direct suggestions, from without, *foris non intus*.[1] Furthermore, many exegetes insisted that the accounts of the temptation given by the Evangelists show that this was the way he went about his business: he spoke to Christ and Christ answered him; he said, "Command *these* stones," which implies that he was holding or pointing to real rocks; he asked the Lord to worship him by "bodily gestures"; he carried him to the high mountain and the temple; and was finally ordered to go away.[2] Again, "the text saith, *He came*; which properly signifies some corporeal access."[3] Finally, since he had tempted Adam "outwardly," in the body of the serpent, it was obviously fitting that he should approach the Second Adam in the same manner.[4] But in what form would he choose to appear? His own, or a more attractive one?

The belief that the devil could approach prospective victims under the cover of some pleasing shape was a very ancient one, backed by the highest authority. Not only had he assumed such a shape in order to seduce Adam, but Saint Paul in Second Corinthians speaks of his power to change his ministers into "the ministers of righteousness," and himself into "an angel of light."[5] It was in this disguise that he came to the imprisoned Saint Juliana and tried (unsuccessfully) to persuade her to

---

[1] See Chapter II, pp. 20-21.

[2] T. Taylor, p. 74. See also Knox, 4.106-7; *Assembly's Annotations*, 2. sig. A4ʳ; Bilson, pp. 304-5; Dyke, pp. 275-76; Leigh, p. 9; Maldonatus, col. 87; Manton, pp. 31-32; Chemnitius, p. 41.

[3] Fuller, p. 34. See also Manton, p. 31.

[4] T. Taylor, p. 74; Pareus, p. 65; Perkins, p. 33; Lapide, p. 101; Chemnitius, p. 41.

[5] II Corinthians 2:14-15.

save herself by renouncing her faith.[6] He frequently appeared
to the desert fathers as an elegant young man, a beautiful
woman, or even Christ himself.[7]

It was therefore quite possible to conclude that when he
tempted the Lord, he put on some innocent and engaging form
to conceal his identity and make his suggestions more plausible.
If such a tradition existed during the Middle Ages, however,
it must have been a very weak one, for no writer I have consulted mentions it, and no artist depicts Satan arguing with
Christ except in his own shape, dark, malign, and hideous.[8]
From the fourteenth century to the eighteenth, on the other
hand, both writers and artists frequently assume that Satan
came to the wilderness in disguise. The new tradition never
completely superseded the older one that the devil went about
his work quite openly;[9] nor did it ever achieve a fixed and
definite form. In the first place, there was no general agreement
as to *what* disguise Satan chose to adopt. Some expositors say
quite frankly that it is impossible to tell.[10] Others content themselves with stating merely that he took a " human " shape.[11]

---

[6] " *Life of Saint Juliana*," *Acta SS.* of the Bollandists, vol. 2, February, quoted
in A. N. Didron, *Christian Iconography*, 2.127-28.

[7] J. Levron, *Le Diable dans l'Art* (Paris, 1935), p. 18.

[8] See for instance: *Gospel Book of Otto* (10th century) fol. 52, in the Cathedral
Treasury at Aachen, reproduced in Beissel, *Hs. Kaisers Otto* (1886), pl. VII; Illustrated ms. (11th century), Bremen: Lib. Stadbibl., b. 21; Fresco at Brinay, Ch.,
Aignan, choir (12th century), reproduced in *Gaz. B. A.*, 56 (1914), figs. p. 227 and
229; Sculpture " dans un chapiteau de Saulieu en Bourgogne " (12th century),
reproduced in Levron, p. 34; two windows at Chartres Cathedral (12th-13th century). The temptation is seldom or never represented in art prior to the ninth
century. — (Detzel, 1.256).

[9] Satan is not in disguise in an engraving of the temptation by the L Cz master
(end of 15th century), reproduced by E. Bock, p. 183; or in one woodcut and two
engravings of the same subject from the extra-illustrated Kitto Bible in the Huntingdon Library: see Plate I. Many theologians (*e. g.*, Knox, Calvin, Marlorate,
Poole, Wild, Cajetanus, and Andrewes) say nothing of the devil's appearing in
disguise; while Woodhead writes: " Perhaps not disguising at all who he was (which
also was well known to our Lord,) [he] subtilly desired some evidence of the super-
eminent Dignity of our Lords person, as it were for his own satisfaction, and that
he might know his due subjection to him." — p. 114.

[10] B. Aretius, *Commentarii in Evangelium Secundum Lucam* (Lansanne, 1596),
pp. 126-27; T. Taylor, p. 75; Fuller, pp. 34-35. Perkins (p. 33), writes only that
" he came in some bodily shape," as do Blackwood, p. 93; Cradock, p. 39; and
Chemnitius, p. 41.

[11] Jansen, col. 531; Ludolphus of Saxony, p. 79; Pareus, pp. 65-66; *Assembly's
Annotations*, 2. sig. A4[r]; Piscator, p. 48; Lapide, p. 101; Leigh, p. 9; and Maldo-

Artists and writers who actually depict him under the shape represent him variously as:

1) *a benevolent old hermit,* clad in a monkish robe, often equipped with a rosary. This is the disguise most commonly ascribed to him, perhaps because it was thought the one in which he could best hope to deceive Christ. His age and holiness would naturally win his victim's confidence and immediate respect, while his calling would make his appearance in the wilderness entirely plausible.[12]

2) *an old man of mean appearance,* as in the *Christiados* of Alexander Ross:

> Terribili squalore senis, cui plurima mento
> Canicies inculta jacet, stant lumina flamma;
> Sordidus ex humero nodo dependet amictus,
> Et frontem obscoenam rugis arat, ignea torquens
> Lumina tum tremulo tendens per gramina gressu
> Pestiferas aperit fauces, & voces superba
> Assatur coeli Regum — [13]

3) *an old man, richly dressed.* Since I have seen only one instance of this disguise, it may be simply a variant on the ordinary "old man" shape.[14]

4) *a handsome young man,* a disguise probably suggested by the "angel of light" passage in Second Corinthians.[15]

natus, col. 87, who makes the interesting comment that it must have been human, for the Evangelists would have described it if it were unusual disguise, like the serpent-form in Genesis.

[12] Woodcut, *Bibel Froschzauer* (1551), fol. CLXXXIII[v] and fol. CCXIIII[v] (duplicates); Woodcut illustrating Justus Jonas's *Catechismus,* reproduced by Burton in his edition of "*Cranmer's*" *Catechism,* p. 142; Jan Van Londerseel, *Landscape with the Temptation of Christ,* after David Verick-Boons (1578-1629), print in the Baltimore Museum of Art; Sandro Botticelli, *The Temptation of Christ,* in the "Cleansing of the Leper" fresco in the Sistine Chapel (1481-82), reproduced in E. M. Phillipps, *The Frescoes in the Sixtine Chapel* (London, 1901), pp. 27-28; Engraving, illustrating *L'Histoire du Vieux et du Nouveau Testament de Sieur de Royaumont* (17th century), reproduced in Levron, p. 93; Seven woodcuts and engravings of uncertain dates in the extra-illustrated Kitto Bible: see Plate II. See also Bale, sig. D1[v]; Fletcher, 1. 43-45; Luca, col. 531; Xavier, p. 129. Fuller (pp. 34-35) and T. Taylor (pp. 74-75), list the theory, but reject it.

[13] Ross, p. 256. Seven engravings in the extra-illustrated Kitto Bible show Satan in the same disguise: see Plate III.

[14] Engraving by Dirick Jacobzoon Vellert (Dirick Van Star) (1525), reproduced in H. Gilhofer and H. Ranschburg's *An Important Collection of Fine and Rare Engravings and Woodcuts* (N. p., [192-]), p. 114.

[15] Titian, painting of "The Temptation of Christ [1530]," reproduced by Henniker-

5) *Three different shapes, one for each temptation.* In 1537, Martin Luther preached a sermon in which he equated the temptations of Christ with the temptations of his Church at various periods of its history. While it was poor and persecuted, Satan attacked it in an ugly dark form, threatening it with death and torture. Later, when it was torn by controversy, he appeared in the form of an angel of light, twisting the Scriptures to his purpose, as he does at the temptation of the tower. Finally, when it became rich and prosperous, he came as the Prince of this World, to corrupt it by power and wealth.[15a] Luther does not say in so many words that the devil tempted Christ in these three specific disguises; he seems to have been simply trying to indicate in symbolic terms the differing character of the three temptations. So were the authors of the *Assembly's Annotations* when they wrote of the temptation of the kingdoms that Satan "cometh not now like a friend to advise, as verse 3 or like a divine to direct, as verse 6, but like a Monarch to seduce our Saviour with great gifts"; and Manton when he observed of the same episode that "before he appeared as a Friend to advise him in his hunger; then as a Divine to instruct him how to discover himself as the *Messiah*; now as a plaine usurper of Gods worship."[16] This sort of comment, however, could very easily pass into a tradition that Satan really did appear in three such shapes; and we have some evidence that that is what happened. A German engraving in the extra-illustrated Kitto Bible shows him carrying out the temptation of bread as an ugly, dark man; the temptation of the tower as an angel; and the temptation of the kingdoms as a sort of Pope, in full ecclesiastical regalia.[17] Moreover, Lapide, who writes

---

Heaton, *The Temptation of Christ by Tiziano Vecelli called Titian* (New York, 1925), p. 5. See also an engraving in the extra-illustrated Kitto Bible: Plate IV. Manton (p. 34) says that Satan appeared "visibly in the shape of an Angel of Light." John Lightfoot (3. 42) also states that the devil came "in the shape of an angel," but since he immediately adds that "so had Eve been deceived in him, mistaking him for a good angel," he may mean no more than that Satan took on some innocent and attractive form, not necessarily an angelic one.

[15a] Luther, 45. 28-36, *passim*.

[16] *Assembly's Annotations*, 2. sig. A4ᵛ; Manton, p. 130. Aretius (*Commentarii in Evangelium Secundum Marcum*, p. 43) and Johannes Coccejus (*Scholia in Matthaeum, Opera Omnia* [Amstelodami, 1675], 4. 9) both note that Satan "formavit se in Angelum lucis" at the temptation of the tower, though neither implies that he took any other shape or that this one was actually a disguise.

[17] See Plate V.

that Satan arrived on the scene in a human shape, adds, when he comes to the temptation of the tower:

Neque hic se prodidit daemon, quia velut Angelus lucis Christum transferre poterat, aut certe non multum se hoc raptu prodi curabat diabolus, qui se iam suspectum, imò perspectum esse Christo, suspicabatur & metuebat. Unde in tertia tentatione volens adorari à Christo, plane omnem Angeli lucis laruam deposuit, seseque ac satanicam suam arrogantiam detexit.[18]

It is clear, therefore, that a Renaissance artist or writer could (if he wished) present Satan in three different forms, though there was no general agreement as to just what these were: either an ugly man or a "friend"; either a divine or an angel; and either a prince or simply himself.

In general, however, both artists and writers preferred to suppose that Satan did not attempt more than one disguise. Some assumed that he retained it throughout the temptation.[19] Others were more inclined to think that he cast it aside before or after his final failure.[20] Still others seem to have been of the opinion that he gave it up immediately after the temptation of bread: perhaps they reasoned that, since the disguise was intended merely to deceive, there was no point in his maintaining it any longer, since he could hardly have hoped to make Christ believe that a friendly hermit or an elderly peasant was capable of carrying him through the air to distant cities and mountaintops.[21]

[18] Lapide, p. 103.

[19] Two engravings in the extra-illustrated Kitto Bible: see Plate VI. Bale, Ludolphus, Luca, Xavier, Ross, Jansen, Taylor, Fletcher, and Lightfoot apparently believed that he kept his disguise to the end, for they do not say that he cast it off at any point in the proceedings.

[20] The great Botticelli fresco in the Sistine Chapel shows him tearing away his monk's gown with a gesture of impotent rage, revealing a hideous furry body beneath it, as he plunges past Christ over the brink of the mountain. In the "*Cranmer*" *Catechism* woodcut, he is seen in disguise at the first two temptations, but falling from the tower in his own shape at the last one. Cf. Lapide, above, p. 46.

[21] See Jerome Wierix, *The Temptation of Christ* (1680-81), print, after a painting by Bernardino Passeri, in the Baltimore Museum of Art; the Van Londerseel *Landscape with the Temptation of Christ*; the woodcut in the *Bibel Froschzauer*; and three engravings in the extra-illustrated Kitto Bible: cf. Plate II. All show Satan in disguise at the first temptation, and in his own shape at the second and third. In five other illustrations from the Kitto Bible, the figures in one of the final temptations are too small to be distinguished; but Satan appears disguised at the first, and undisguised at the one where he can be identified: see Plate IV. The presence of this undisguised Satan is sometimes all that shows that the Satan

A tradition so vague, so unfixed, and so confusing left every writer free to do very much what he pleased with it. He was at liberty to decide what disguise Satan adopted, whether he altered it, and how long he retained it. He might treat the subject according to one of the many tentative patterns devised by his predecessors, or he might invent a new pattern of his own. Milton chose to invent a pattern of his own.

His Satan comes to the wilderness, conventionally enough, in the form of

> an aged man in rural weeds,
> Following, as seem'd, the quest of some stray ewe,
> Or wither'd sticks to gather, which might serve
> Against a winter's day when winds blow keen,
> To warm him wet return'd from field at eve.[22]

Milton may have found this particular disguise readymade in the tradition; or he may have worked it out for himself. It answers the devil's purposes much better than the more familiar and widely accepted one of the friendly hermit. As a simple, poverty-stricken old man, with no particular pretensions to sanctity, he can dwell on the terrors and evils of Christ's situation with an energy that would be highly unbecoming in a pious recluse, who is presumably in the desert from choice. His concern for the Lord's immediate physical welfare (and his own) is, under the circumstances, completely natural and even appealing: it does not excite the suspicion it might if he were pretending to be a devout ascetic, above the concerns of this

---

of the first temptation is in disguise at all. In order clearly to identify a disguised Satan as the devil, artists very often provided him with distinctive iconographical attributes, such as horns, hoofs, wings, or claws (see Plates II, IV, and VI). When the disguise is as obvious as it is in Plate II, there is no difficulty in perceiving the artist's intentions; but when it consists simply of a human face and a nondescript garment (as in Plate IV), it would be hard to tell whether the devil is in disguise or not, if he did not appear naked and undisguised at one or both of the other temptations. During the Renaissance (especially after the Council of Trent excluded horrible and unseemly works of art from the churches), it became more and more conventional to portray Satan as an ordinary human being, usually clothed, and distinguished only by such appropriate physical peculiarities as a small pair of wings or horns. — (Levron, pp. 91-92). It follows that when an artist chooses to depict only one of the temptations, it is frequently impossible to say whether he intends to present an undisguised Satan, or a Satan in disguise with distinctive iconographical attributes to identify him. Two of the illustrations in the Kitto Bible fall into this category: see Plate VII.

[22] *P. R.*, 1. 314-18.

world. Hence, if Milton ever seriously entertained the notion of presenting Satan in the hermit disguise—and it was so popular that he may well have known and considered it—he may have given it up because he thought the peasant-disguise better and more plausible.

Christ detects and exposes the imposture at once. Curiously enough, Milton is the only writer I have encountered, with the exception of Lapide, who apparently gave any serious attention to this particular problem. Giles Fletcher notes after the first temptation that " well knewe our Saviour this the Serpent was ";[23] but his Christ does not tell Satan that he recognizes him. Ludolphus, Xavier, Jansen, Pareus, Ross, Piscator, Leigh, Maldonatus, and Thomas Taylor simply state that the devil came into the wilderness in some human shape, and then drop the whole question. The impression one receives is that they merely attached the disguise-tradition to the existing tradition, and let it go at that, without attempting to integrate the two, or to solve the problems raised by the introduction of the new motif. The artists who depicted Satan disguised at the first temptation and undisguised at the second and third seem to have worked out the implications of the theme more fully. Unless one assumes that Satan either came in the shape of an angel or shifted his disguise, he could not have been trying to impose on Christ's credulity when he carried him bodily through the air to the temple and the high mountain. Therefore, he must have known that Christ knew who he was. Therefore, Christ must have told him he knew, presumably at the first temptation. And even if one did assume that Satan came as an angel, the proper procedure was obviously still to make it clear that the Lord detected and could unmask him, as Milton's Christ does.

Milton's Satan, however, though he gives up any attempt to conceal his identity, does not immediately resume his own form. When he leaves the Lord at the end of the first day, he is still a " gray dissimulation ";[24] and when he returns at the beginning of the second, he is " a man . . . / Not rustic as before, but seemlier clad, / As one in city, or court, or palace bred." [25] He has apparently altered his style to suit his material: a richly

[23] Fletcher, 1. 47.   [24] *P. R.*, 1. 498.   [25] *P. R.*, 2. 298-300.

dressed courtier accompanies the splendors of the banquet and
the glories of the world much better than an unkempt peasant.
Unfortunately, however, the term "man" is rather ambiguous:
one cannot be sure whether Milton means that he has come
back as a completely different person, or as the gray dissimulation of the previous evening, in a costume better suited to
the character of the suggestions he is about to make.

It is still more difficult to understand how he is supposed to
look on the third day, when he emerges from the woods "in
wonted shape."[26] "Wonted shape" may mean "the shape he
usually wears," or, in other words, his own shape, with no
attempt at disguise. This would be entirely natural and fitting.
Since Satan's object is now to cow and overwhelm the Lord
rather than to win him, it is no longer necessary or effective to
keep up the mask of ancient innocence or worldly sophistica-
tion proper to the preceding temptations. On the contrary,
it is very much more to the purpose to drop all pretence, and
let Christ see him as he really is, with the full force of his personal ugliness, malignity, and power to back up the terrors of
his threats and brutalities. If this reading of "wonted" is the
correct one, it is probable that Milton, like Lapide and the
unknown artist of the Kitto engraving, thought that the devil
shifted his shape at each appearance to correspond to the
nature of the business he had in hand. In that case, I think it
very unlikely that the "courtier" of the second day is the
"aged man" of the first, with finer clothes and suppler man-
ners. Three distinct forms, one for each occasion, make a clear
and symmetrical pattern. Why disturb the balance by carrying
a form devised for one occasion half-way over into another?

On the other hand, "wonted shape" may mean no more
than "the shape in which he usually appeared in the wilderness." In that case, the "courtier" of the second day must be
the "aged man" of the first, for there would be no point in
referring to the devil's *accustomed* shape, if he had actually
assumed more than one. If this definition of "wonted" is right,
Milton must have meant to imply that Satan adopted only a
single bodily form, and retained it to the end, though he altered
his dress and manner to accord with the character of his pro-

[26] *P. R.*, 4. 449.

posals. So brief and vague an account of his appearance is suitable enough as a casual allusion to a matter already established; one would expect a good writer to go to greater lengths and take more pains if he were really describing something new and startling, like Satan's unexpected resumption of his own awful personality. Furthermore, he states that when the devil took Christ to the temple, "he caught him up, and *without* wing, / Of Hippogrif bore through the Air sublime." [27] This suggests that Satan is still an aged man: he is winged when he appears in *Paradise Lost* and in much Renaissance art. But even if the phrase "without wing" refers to the devil instead of the hippogrif (which is by no means certain), the point is still far from being conclusive: the undisguised Satan was frequently represented without his wings in Milton's day; [28] and it may well have been a figure of this sort which the poet had in mind. On the whole, however, I think "wonted shape" makes better sense if it is interpreted as "usual disguise" rather than "ordinary form." But either interpretation is possible; and both have the support of the tradition. The question thus becomes one which every reader must decide for himself.

[27] *P. R.*, 4. 541-42.
[28] See Plates I and II.

CHAPTER V

THE TRIPLE EQUATION

A reviewer discussing Clunaic art in a recent issue of the London *Times Literary Supplement* observes that on the Puerta de las Plasterias of the cathedral of Santiago, a picture of the Fall of Man is balanced not by its usual antithesis in the New Testament, the Crucifixion, but by an abbreviated representation of the temptation of Christ. "Here," he adds,

> we find the idea which centuries later was implicitly expressed in Milton's *Paradise Regained* — namely, that Christ's victory over Satan was actually accomplished when he bade the tempter to get behind him and to depart. It is, of course, not feasible that Milton had any knowledge of the author whose christological speculations the Spanish sculptor was made to follow.[1]

That a Spanish sculptor and an English poet who lived centuries later should both have read the same book by the same writer does, indeed, seem wildly improbable. But it does not necessarily follow that Milton must therefore have remained unaware of the nature of such "christological speculations" about the temptation. Long before either he or the Spanish sculptor were born, the hypothesis that Adam's failure was counterbalanced by the triumph of Christ had become so established and familiar a point of doctrine that the impossibility of tracing the work of poet and artist to a common source results simply from the multiplicity and the agreement of the sources available to both.

As we have already seen, medieval and Renaissance theologians generally assume that Christ undertook the temptation primarily to restore to man that capacity to resist it of which Adam's surrender had deprived him. The Fathers of the Church frequently go even further and make the analogy between the two events as exact and specific as possible. They argue that the three sins which Christ refused to commit were, in essence, the same three which had caused Adam's fall: gluttony, vain

---

[1] Anon. "The Spirit of Cluny." Review of Werner Weisbach's *Religiose Reform und Mittelalterliche Kunst. TLS* (April 6, 1946), p. 158.

glory, and avarice. Adam, of course, actually signifies Adam-
and-Eve, who, to facilitate comparison with Christ, are considered as one individual, "Adam" comprehending "Eve" in
the same way that the term "man" at its broadest compre-
hends "woman." The devil, then, had tempted Adam to yield
to gluttony by showing him that the fruit of the tree was good
for food and pleasant to the eyes (*ex gula quippe tentavit cum
cibum ligni vetitum ostendit, atque ad comedendum suasit*).
In exactly the same manner, he tempted Christ to yield to
gluttony by suggesting that he turn the stones to bread to
satisfy his appetite (*per gulam quippe tentat cum dicit: "Dic
ut lapides isti panes fiant"*). Again, he won Adam and Eve
through vain glory when he promised them that they should
be as gods (*"Eritis sicut dii"*); and he tried to so win Christ
when he suggested that he presume on his divine powers and
fling himself from the pinnacle that he might be acknowledged
the Son of God (*per vanam gloriam tentat cum dicit: "Si Filium
Dei es, mitte te deorsum"*). Lastly, he excited the avarice of
Adam and Eve by telling them that they would know good
and evil (*"Scientes boni et malum"*), since the sin of avarice
may consist not only in the desire for wealth, but in the thirst
for mere power. He hoped that Christ would fall into the same
trap when he offered him all the might, honor, riches, and
glory of the world at the temptation of the kingdoms (*per sub-
limitatis avaritiam tentat cum regna omnia mundi ostendit,
dicens: "Haec omnia tibi dabo"*).[2]

Furthermore, the Fathers argued, since Luke states that all
the temptations were completed when only three had actually
taken place,[3] it followed (as Bede explains) that "videlicet his
omnium vitiorum origines amplectuntur et fontes. Joanne attes-

---

[2] St. Gregory the Great, cols. 1135-36. See also St. Ambrose, *Expositionis in
Lucam*, cols. 1697-1706, *passim*; Bede, *In Matthaei Evangelium Expositio*, col. 20;
Pseudo-Jerome, col. 559; Walafridus Strabus, *Expositio in Quatuor Evangelia*, col.
870; Rabanus Maurus, *In Matthaeum*, cols. 784-85. Euthymius Zigabenus (col.
175); St. Bruno Astensius (col. 91); and Rupertus Abbas (*In Quatuor Evangelistarum Commentariorum Liber Unus, Patr. Lat.* 167. col. 1548) state that Christ
and Adam were both tempted with gluttony, but do not carry the comparison
further. The analogy is also given in full by such minor medieval writers as the
authors of *Twelfth Century Homilies*, pp. 99-100; *A Stanzaic Life of Christ*, ed.
E. A. Foster (London, 1926), p. 176; and *The Chester Plays*, ed. H. Deimling
(London, 1892), pp. 224-25.

[3] Luke 4:13.

tante qui ait: *Quia omne quod in mundo est, concupiscentia carnis est et concupiscentia oculorum, et superbia vitae* [I John 2: 16]." Bede then goes on to add that in the parable of the supper [Luke 14: 15-24], the excuses of the three guests represent the three types of sin described by John and illustrated by the temptations of Christ. The man who refuses to come because he has been married is guilty of "uxor appetitus," which is the same thing as gluttony, and stands for *concupiscentia carnis*. The man who would rather go "prove" his new yoke of oxen is guilty of vain glory, or *concupiscentia oculorum*. And the man who prefers to attend to the field he has just purchased is guilty of avarice, or *superbia vitae*.[4] In other words, by overcoming gluttony, vain glory, and avarice, Christ might be said to have overcome all temptation, because all are mere variants of the three basic seductions typified by gluttony, vain glory, and avarice: concupisence of the flesh, concupisence of the eye, and the pride of life: the flesh, the world, and the devil.[5] The three are arranged on a sort of ascending scale of potency, beginning with the lowest and most venial, and ending with the highest and most deadly.

The addition of this second set of parallels to the first one results in a sort of triple equation between the temptations of Adam, the temptations of Christ, and all the temptations of this world. As summarized above, it is postulated on the basis of the order of temptations given by Matthew. But it was also possible to postulate it on the basis of the order given by Luke. This entailed more than simply transposing the second and third factors of the equation, since it was desirable to keep the three sins in the proper succession: flesh, world, devil: bad, worse, worst. "Avarice" and "vain glory," however, are rather anomalous sins: it was quite possible to call the temptation of the kingdoms, the temptation of the world (*concupiscentia oculorum*), and the temptation of the tower, the temptation of the devil (*superbia vitae*). The Luke equation, in fact,

---

[4] Bede, *In Lucae Evangelium Expositio*, col. 370. For less elaborate presentations of the same theory, see St. Ambrose, *Expositionis in Lucam*, cols. 1701-2; Chrysostom, cols. 212-13; Theophylactus, *Enarratio in Evangelium Lucae*, col. 747; St. Thomas Aquinas, *Summa Theologica*, pars 3, quaest. 41, art. 4.

[5] Ludolphus of Saxony (p. 79) specifically describes the sins as those of the flesh, the world, and the devil.

actually made better sense than the Matthew: the *regna omnia mundi* is a more obvious and suitable temptation of the world than the *mitte te deorsum*, while the *mitte te deorsum* conforms to Satan's original offence—desire for vain glory, presumption in aspiring to be as God—much more closely than the *regna omnia mundi*. But because the Matthew order dominated the tradition and commentators wished to keep the three sins in the right sequence, the Matthew equation was the one generally accepted and used.[6]

Here and there, of course, one finds slight variations from the standard form. St. Thomas Aquinas, for instance, suggests a different set of texts from Genesis as the *loci* of Adam's temptations. He thinks the persuasion of vain glory came with the words: "then your eyes shall be opened,"[7] perhaps because they so directly imply the presence of *concupiscentia oculorum*; and he assigns the full clause which follows — "And ye shall be as gods, knowing good and evil " — to the temptation of power or "extremam superbiam," perhaps because he is working with the Matthew order and feels that such an arrangement links the original offence of Satan to the equation more firmly than the other.[8] Pseudo-Chrysostom and St. Hilary likewise describe the *regna omnia mundi* as a temptation of ambition corresponding to the promise that Adam and Eve shall be as gods, while Chrysostom associates the *mitte te deorsum* with the flattery that their eyes shall be opened.[9] But such deviations from the norm are comparatively insignificant, and do not affect the main structure of the triple equation.

The triple equation did much to support and explain the hypothesis that Christ submitted to the devil's attacks in order to show his followers how best to overcome them. Since each of his temptations stands for a whole class of temptations, and represents all that fall within that class, there was therefore no *fraus diaboli* which could not be referred to one of those practised on Christ, or could not be overcome by observing or fol-

---

[6] The Luke equation is, however, given by Walafridus Strabus (*Glossa Ordinaria*, *Patr. Lat.* 114. col. 254), and by St. Paschasius Radbertus (col. 107).

[7] Genesis 3:5.

[8] St. Thomas Aquinas, *Summa Theologica*, pars 3, quaest. 41, art. 4.

[9] Pseudo-Chrysostom, [*Sermon on Matthew 4: 6-8*], *Patr. Gr.* 61. cols. 686-88; St. Hilary, *Commentarius in Matthaeum*, col. 930; Chrysostom, col. 211. None of the three gives a full equation.

lowing his example. The carnal sinner might learn from the temptation of bread to curb his appetites and mortify the flesh, in the remembrance that man does not live by it alone, and that if "we love betere Goddis word þan ony mete þat we shulden ete, we shulden not leve Goddis word and chese þis mete." [10] The worldly soul might learn from the temptation of the tower that he was in grave danger of tempting God by ostentation and presumption. [11] The proud and powerful might learn from the temptation of the kingdoms that they must never pursue ambition to the point of worshipping the devil:

Quos enim alios per istos intelligamus, nisi imperatores, reges, duces, principes, caeterosque saeculi hujus potentes, quos in montem excelsum, id est in ipsarum dignitatem sublimitatem per homicidia, perjuria, furta, rapinas, proditiones, fraudes, et caetera hujus modi diabolus ducit et exaltat? Ex isti quidem eum adorant, eum colunt et venerantur . . . neque enim et audiunt hoc quod dicit Dominus Jesus. [12]

By the same token, the forty days of fasting which preceded the three assaults of the devil could be considered a demonstration of the merits and desirability of corporal abstinence, reinforcing the lesson of the first temptation. According to St. Ambrose:

Unde et Dominus Jesus volens nos adversus diaboli tentamenta fortiores reddere, certaturos jejunavit; ut sciremus quia aliter illecebras mali non possumus vincere. Denique ipse diabolus primum tentamentorum suorum spiculum de voluptate intorsit, dicens: *Si Filius Dei es, dic ut lapides isti panes fiant.* Unde ait Dominus: *Non in pane solo vivit homo, sed in omni verbo Dei,* et noluit facere cum posset, ut magis lectionis studio quam voluptati intendere nos salutari praecepto doceret. Et quia isti jejundandum negant, qua causa Christus jejunaverit, astruant; nisi ut nobis exemplo esset ejus jejunium. [13]

It was at this point that the leaders of the Reformation parted company with the Fathers of the Church. Much of the Fathers' teaching they could and did take over and use; but the particular exemplary function ascribed to the *quadraginta*

---

[10] Wyclif, 1. 110.   [11] Chrysostom, col. 211.   [12] St. Bruno Astensius, col. 93.
[13] St. Ambrose, *Epistolarum Classis I, Patr. Lat.* 16. cols. 1244-45. For other statements that Christ fasted to set us an example, see Chrysostom, col. 209; Theophylactus, *Enarratio in Evangelium Lucae,* col. 746; St. Paschasius Radbertus, col. 188; St. Gregory the Great, col. 1137.

dies and the first temptation was more than they could accept. The difficulty lay in the fact that the Reformers, though they countenanced and even encouraged certain limited forms of fasting, insisted that such discipline was not meant to merit grace, but simply to keep the body in a suitable condition for the various duties of our calling.[14] It had no value in itself, was not one of the works commanded by God, and hence should neither be extravagantly praised nor rigorously prosecuted.[15] This was a doctrine difficult, if not impossible, to maintain in the face of the contention that the forty-day fast and the first answer to the devil were especially designed by Christ to show his followers the worth and necessity of mere abstinence, *ut sciremus quia aliter illecebras mali non possumus vincere.* It was clear that either the Reformers had erred or the Fathers misinterpreted the text. The Reformers were naturally not long in discovering proof that the Fathers had misinterpreted the text.

In the first place, Calvin argues, Christ certainly did not fast forty days in order to set an example to others. For the power of sustaining life without food for so long a period was plainly superhuman: a manifestation of divinity, undertaken as a sort of introduction to the preaching of the Gospel, a proof that the doctrine to come was not the invention of a man, but a revelation from God.[16] As *sigillum* and *miraculum*, therefore, the fast could only be adored; it neither could nor should be imitated. "Singulare miraculum Deus edidit quum Filium suum exemit a necessitate edendi: anon insana audacia aemulantur Deum qui idem sua virtute affectant?"[17]

The first temptation, however, could not be disposed of in the same manner, since Calvin agreed with the Fathers that Christ had submitted to the attacks of the devil in order to show his followers how they ought to combat them.[18] He did

[14] Ausberg Confession, art. xxxv; quoted in " Fasting," *Cyclopedia of Biblical, Theological, and Ecclesiastical Literature.* 3. 490.

[15] John Calvin, *The Institution of the Christian Religion,* trans. Thomas Norton (London, 1611), pp. 612-13.

[16] *Ibid.,* p. 613.

[17] Calvin, *Commentarii,* p. 51. Fuller puts the matter more bluntly: "Popish superstitious Fasts are good only to fill the bowels with winde, and the heart with pride." — p. 59.

[18] *Ibid.,* p. 51. The Protestants were especially attracted to this hypothesis because it gave them an opportunity to cite Christ's quoting of Scripture as evidence that

not therefore attempt to deny that in this case Christ's example was to be followed; he simply asserted that the Fathers' conception of that example was an erroneous one, based upon a failure to comprehend the true nature and significance of the temptation. It was absurd, he contended, to suppose that Satan tried to trick Jesus into committing the sin of gluttony: no starving man commits the sin of gluttony when he merely eats dry bread in order to satisfy the lawful demands of nature. What the devil really attempted was the destruction of the Lord's *faith*. What he said in effect was: "You thought that God loved and would provide for you; but since He has left you here to perish of hunger in this wilderness, you must now give up your confidence in Him, and provide for your own wants by your own powers." It was in this sense that Christ himself understood Satan's suggestion. If he had thought of it as the Fathers had, he would have retorted with a text stressing the necessity of self-control and sobriety. But he chose instead a verse which is simply an assertion of God's providence:

Non solo pane vivere hominem. acsi diceret, Tu me aliquid remedii excogitare jubes, quo mihi aliter quam permittit Deus, succurram. Atqui hoc diffidentiae esset, cujus nulla est ratio quamdiu promittit Deus se mihi nutritium fore. Tu Satan ejus gratiam pani alligas: ipse vero contra testatur, ut desint omnes cibi, solam suam benedictionem ad nos alendos sufficere.[19]

In other words, Christ knew that, if he turned the stones into bread, his sin would not lie in the actual satisfaction of his hunger, but in the shameful lack of trust which made that satisfaction possible; and his response therefore cannot have been intended to put his followers on their guard against indulging bodily appetite, but only against permitting bodily indigence to drive them into the error of doubting or distrusting the love and wisdom of God. All orthodox Protestant theologians took the same view of the temptation of bread and the *quadraginta dies*.[20]

---

he wanted the Bible in the hands of the laity. See for example, Trapp, p. 52; Blackwood, p. 95; Perkins, pp. 42-43; Thomas Cartwright, *A Confutation of the Rhemists* (N. p., 1618), p. 19.

[19] *Ibid.*, p. 51.

[20] See for example: Andrewes, pp. 492-511; Marlorate, pp. 38-61; T. Taylor, pp. 47-49; Aretius, *Commentarii in Evangelium Secundum Lucam*, pp. 123-28; Francis Roberts, *Clavis Bibliorum* (London, 1675), p. 472; Luther, 45. 25-30; Pareus, pp. 65-

This new version of the *dic ut lapides* necessitated in its turn a certain revision of the old equation between the temptations of Christ, the temptations of Adam, and all the temptations of this life. The Protestants were no less eager than the Catholics to make the most of any correspondence between the three; but since in their eyes the gluttony of the First Man was no longer equivalent to the hunger of the Second, the exact and delicate symmetry of the original balance could be retained only by wrenching the whole into line with the Calvinist view of the first temptation:

As it is true that Paul saith, that Christ resembled Adam, and was made a "quickening spirit," as Adam was a "living soul," . . . so may Christ and Adam be compared in these three temptations. For they were both tempted with " concupisence of the flesh, concupisence of the eye, and pride of life." In Adam the devil first brought him to a conceit that God envied his good, and of purpose kept him hoodwinked lest he should see his good, as we see falconers put hoods over hawks' eyes, to make them more quiet and ruly. Secondly, he lulls him on to a proud conceit of himself, by persuading him that by eating he should be like God. Thirdly, he sheweth the fruit, which was pleasant. So in Christ's temptation: first, he would have brought him to murmur against God; secondly, to presume; and thirdly, to commit idolatry. . . . And under these three heads come all temptations.

To some of these extremes will the devil seek to drive one. First, by distrust he will seek to drive us to use unlawful means for the obtaining of necessary things, as bread is when a man is hungry. Or if we be in no such want, that that temptation cannot take place, then through superfluity he will tempt us to wanton and unnecessary desires, as to throw ourselves down, that the Angels may take us up, and having prevailed so far, then he carrieth us to the devil and all. " All this will I give Thee ": there is his " all." " Fall down and worship me ": there is the devil with it. . . . First he wraps himself in necessity and thereby winds himself in unperceived, then he brings us to make riches our god.[21]

67; Knox, 4. 99-112; Chemnitius, p. 42; Calovius, p. 30; Henry Hammond, p. 20; *Assembly's Annotations*, 2. sig. A4ʳ; Diodate, sec. sig. A3ʳ; *Dutch Annotations*, 2. Cᵛ; Bucer, pp. 92-97; Piscator, p. 49-59, *passim*; Udall, sig. C5ʳ–D4ʳ; Dyke, pp. 228-39; Ward, pp. 89-96; Perkins, pp. 21-47; Mayer, p. 79; Trapp. pp. 51-52; Blackwood, pp. 91-94; Fuller, pp. 20-46; Cradock, p. 39. See also Bale, sigs. D2ᵛ–D3ᵛ, and Fletcher, 1. 45-47. Orthodox Catholics continued to use the medieval interpretation: see for example, Luca, cols. 532-35; I. H., pps. 268-69; Cordier, pp. 46-50, *passim*; Lapide, pp. 99-102; Maldonatus, col. 86. Maldonatus is particularly interesting because he gives a lengthy and stormy rebuttal of Calvin's arguments on the fast.

[21] Andrewes, pp. 496-97. See also T. Taylor, pp. 79; 285; 291. The *Assembly's*

John Lightfoot also presents a complete equation, but postulated on the order in Luke instead of the one in Matthew:

As our mother Eve was tempted by Satan to the "lust of the flesh, the lust of the eyes, and the pride of life," (for she saw that it was good for food, that it was pleasant to the eyes, and to be desired to make one wise) so by these, had it been possible, would the same tempter have overthrown the seed of the woman: for he tempted him to turn stones into bread, so as to satisfy the longing of the flesh; to fall down and worship him, upon the sight of a bewitching object to his eyes; and to fly through the air in pride, and to get glory among men.[22]

As we have already seen, however, Lightfoot explains the order in Luke by supposing that the evangelist arranged his temptations to correspond to those of Adam, while the order given by Matthew is the historically correct one.[23] He therefore continues to use Matthew's order in his own *Harmony of the Gospels*, even though it follows that he is no longer able to keep the three sins in the proper sequence: flesh, world, devil. Manton, though he does not give the argument about the Luke order, treats the subject exactly as Lightfoot does.[24] Dyke and Perkins apparently agreed with Lightfoot and Manton. Their equations are not quite complete (neither points out an exact parallel in Genesis for the *mitte te deorsum* or gives the key text from John in full); but the fact that Perkins calls the *mitte te deorsum* a temptation of "satanicall pride," and Dyke the *regna omnia mundi*, "concupiscence of the eyes" suggests that they too are imposing the Luke equation on the Matthew enumeration of events, since both follow the Matthew order.[25]

Annotations gives the same equation in a much abbreviated form (1. sig. [B1]ᵛ; 2. sig. A4ʳ; 2. sig. J5ʳ). Musculus (pp. 47-52); Cradock (p. 41); and Blackwood (p. 94) equate the temptation of bread with Eve's temptation to distrust, but do not carry the analogy further. Fuller (pp. 135-36) gives the parallels only for the *regna omnia mundi*. Bucer (fols. 96ᵛ and 102ʳ) equates only the *dic ut lapdies* and the *regna omnia mundi* with the corresponding temptations of Adam. Like Aquinas, he gives the full verse, *Eritis sicut dii, scientes bona & mala*, for the Eden temptation of ambition.

[22] Lightfoot, 3. 42.
[23] See Chapter I, p. 7.
[24] Manton, pp. 17; 45-48; 62-69; 133; 140-43. Note that both he and Lightfoot give Genesis 3:8 as the *locus* of Adam's temptations instead of the more conventional texts.
[25] Dyke: *Distrust* (Christ, p. 240; Adam, p. 246; all mankind, p. 246); *Presumption and Vainglory* (Christ, pp. 283-84; Adam, . . . ; all mankind, p. 285); *Ambition*

Moreover, Richard Ward, while he specifically associates the temptation of Christ with that of Adam only once, and then in rather general terms ("wee may observe how he begins with the second *Adam*, as he did with the first, at the Belly "), adds that "the devill comes armed against Christ with a threefold dart; the first is of the belly . . . ; the second of *fame* and credit; the third of *gaine* and profit. The I. is the concupiscence of the flesh: the II. is the pride of life: the III. is the lust of the eyes." [26] Again, since Ward is working with the Matthew gospel, he must mean that the devil's temptation (*superbia vitae*) was the second in order. By this compromise, he and the others retain the more satisfactory equation of Luke without sacrificing the greater historical accuracy of Matthew. The arrangement is not an absolutely perfect one, but it was probably the best that could be done under the circumstances.

If either form of the Protestant equation is compared point for point with the older one devised by the Fathers, it will be observed that the Protestant theologian usually alters not only the Catholic version of Adam's first temptation, but that of his *avaritia* too. The one change apparently led to the other. In order to square Adam's experience with that of Christ, he was forced to assume that Adam's first temptation was one of doubt or distrust. But the text traditionally associated with that temptation — "The tree was good for food and pleasant to the eyes " [27] — hardly admitted of any such interpretation; it sounded rather as if the physical attractiveness of the fruit proved too much for Adam's appetite. The single phrase "good for food " might pass, for the first temptation was still regarded as that of the flesh. But since Christ's was one of pure necessity, not of pleasure, the element of pleasure had somehow to be completely dissociated from Adam's, if the Protestant was to draw any parallel between the two at all. The simplest way out of the difficulty was to contend that "pleasant to the eyes " actually described the temptation of avarice (and thus could have nothing to do with the first). In the finished equation,

---

(Christ, p. 315; Adam, p. 317; all mankind, p. 317). Perkins: *Distrust* (Christ, p. 33; Adam, p. 34; all mankind, p. 34); *Vainglory* (Christ, p. 65; Adam, . . . ; all mankind, p. 68); *Ambition* (Christ, pp. 91 and 99; Adam, p. 91; all mankind, p. 95).

[26] Ward, p. 96.   [27] Genesis 3:6.

therefore, we find the *cibus ligni vetitus* set up in the place of
the *scientes bonum et malum*, and regarded not so much as
fruit for which Adam hungered as a "pleasant" object which
he desired, an earthly splendor analogous to Christ's "glories"
and man's "temptations of the world or devil."

The application of this particular text to Adam's *avaritia* in
its turn affected Protestant analysis of the temptation of the
kingdoms. The Fathers and their followers were hopelessly
split on the question whether the word "kingdoms" was to be
taken in its allegorical or its literal sense, some arguing that by
"kingdoms" Satan meant merely wealth, power, fame, or other
appropriate glories of the world;[28] some contending that the
"kingdoms" were actual realms, and the glories of the world
pleasures or advantages to be derived from ruling them.[29]
Neither party, however, implied that they were luxuries of a
sort which immediately gratify the body itself. The unlawful
delights of the flesh were already adequately typified by the
"gluttony" of the *dic ut lapides*.[30] Furthermore, the *regna
omnia mundi* was considered a temptation of pure ambition,
of greed for power, corresponding to Adam's desire to be as
God or to know good and evil. The offerings of Satan are
therefore described simply as those which best satisfy the sense
of mastery: rule over vast countries, possession of great riches,
unbounded influence on the hearts and minds of all wicked men.
The Protestant theologians, on the other hand, were committed
to the view that Adam's final sin lay in his desire for a beautiful
object which was also a direct source of physical pleasure. They
were, moreover, unable to deal with the unlawful delights of
the flesh under the heading of the *dic ut lapides*, which in their
eyes referred only to what Jeremy Taylor called "the instances
and first necessities of nature."[31] And yet it was obviously
both essential and desirable that Christ should overcome (and
show his followers how they too might overcome) such important and unmistakable temptations as gluttony, lechery, drunk-

[28] Origen, cols. 1877-79; Bede, *In Matthaei Evangelium Expositio*, col. 20; Walafridus Strabus, *Expositio in Quatuor Evangelia*, col. 870.

[29] Euthymius Zigabenus, cols. 178-79; Pseudo-Chrysostom, cols. 680-88; Theophylactus, col. 182.

[30] Cf. the citation from Bede (on p. 53, above), in which he equates the "gluttony" of the first temptation with the "lechery" of the husband in the parable.

[31] J. Taylor, p. 149.

enness, and the like. The only possible solution was to attach such temptations to the *regna omnia mundi*, and suggest that the glories of the world were such as to excite bodily appetite as well as the more conventional longing for honor, wealth, dominion, and power. Dyke, for instance, points out that the mere sight of an attractive object is often too much for the weak soul, and after listing riches, glory, and office as examples, adds:

for intemperance of appetite, witnesse *Eve, Gen. 3 she saw the fruit was pleasant*; for adultery, *David, Potiphar's wife*, and innumerable moe. . . . Lusting and looking, in Greek differ but in one vowell. For drunkennesse that of Solomon. . . . Get that same Stoicall eye of our Saviour, that we may see eye pleasing and tempting objects, and not be moved and set agogge." [32]

Dyke does not say in so many words that the devil actually showed Christ the equivalent of Solomon's liquor or David's Bathsheba; but Mayer is more direct: he observes that if the kingdoms were allegorical, they would be "kingdomes of gluttony, lechery, pride, &c." [33] The devil in Bale's *Temptation of Our Lord*, after enumerating the actual regions he is prepared to hand over to Christ, and dwelling on "their ryches, their honor, their wealth," goes on to persuade him that

> Here are fayre women, of countenaunce ameable,
> With all kyndes of meates, to the body dylectable.[34]

Similarly, Giles Fletcher, who describes the temptation of the kingdoms allegorically, as a house with four stories, places wine and alluring ladies on the first floor, with "[pleasure in] avarice" and "[pleasure in] ambitious honour" [35] in ascending order on the second and third. The stress laid on the beauty or opulence of the food, the drink, and the females does something to make them appropriate glories of the world, and to conceal the basic incongruity and absurdity of continuing to think of the *dic ut*

[32] Dyke, pp. 317-18. See also Udall, sigs. H1r–H2r; Trapp, p. 38.
[33] Mayer, p. 81. See also Manton, who writes, "Here [Satan] doth ask and promise things glorious, and profitable, and *pleasing to carnal sense* (p. 137). . . . Serious thoughts of the frailty of all sublunary enjoyments [will] keep us modest in what we have, or desire to have, that we may not be blinded with *the delusions of the Flesh*, and enchanted with an admiration of worldly felicity (p. 150)." Italics mine.
[34] Bale, sig. E2r.   [35] Fletcher, 1. 49-56.

lapides as the formal "temptation of the flesh," while treating the chief sins of that flesh in a different category under another heading.

Some Protestant writers, however, do not take the trouble of presenting a triple equation, or working out all its implications: they simply alter the interpretation of the *quadraginta dies* and the temptation of bread, and leave the temptation of the kingdoms as it stands in the Fathers.[36] David Pareus even wishes to discard any form of equation except a bare statement of the fact that Satan made light of God's word in both the garden and the wilderness:

Habere quidem omnes aliquid cognationes cum prima tentatione hominis, non tamen eam, quam aliqui veterum faciunt, quasi prima gulae, altera vanae gloriae, tertia avaritiae fuerit: sed hanc potius, quod ut olim serpens calumniabatur Dei interdictum, quasi nullum, vel iniquum esset, & Deum de throno dejiceret, ita hic Tentator calumniatur vocem coelestem, quod Christus esset filius Dei, quasi fuisset mera impostura, ut Christum quidem praecipitaret.[37]

But since Milton was working on a poem deliberately designed as a sequel and companion-piece to *Paradise Lost*, it was natural and perhaps inevitable that he should make some form of the triple equation the center of *Paradise Regained*.

Though no longer a member of any particular sect, Milton still belonged to the Protestant camp; and *Paradise Regained* is a Protestant poem. The soliloquy on Christ's hunger which immediately precedes the banqueting scene faithfully reflects the Reformers' opinion of the *quadraginta dies*:

> that Fast
> To Vertue I impute not, or count part
> Of what I suffer here; if Nature need not,
> Or God support Nature without repast
> Though needing, what praise is it to endure?[38]

Again, as Professor Gilbert has already observed, the conception of the first temptation is in complete harmony with that of Calvin:[39] Satan implies that "an ill chance" has brought Christ to a place where nothing awaits him but a painful and

---

[36] Marlorate, pp. 64-66; Aretius, *Commentarii in Evangelium Secundum Lucam*, pp. 128-29; Jeremy Taylor, pp. 150-52; Calvin, *Commentarii*, p. 53; etc.
[37] Pareus, p. 66. [38] *P. R.*, 2. 241-51. [39] Gilbert, pp. 604-5.

lingering death, scouts the possibility that he will receive assistance or guidance, and finally insists that he use his own
power to save himself—a speech the implications of which are
summed up by the Lord's stern question: "Why dost thou
then suggest to me distrust?"[40]

This acceptance of the Protestant form of the first temptation entailed the acceptance of the Protestant form of the triple
equation. It was unnecessary for Milton to present that equation systematically and all of a piece, as Andrewes had: he knew
that when a reader brought up on seventeenth-century doctrine
opened the book to find God the Father assuring the angels
that Christ shall win "by Conquest what the first man lost /
By fallacy surpriz'd," and that "his weakness shall o'ercome
Satanic strength / And all the world, and mass of sinful flesh,"[41]
that reader could be trusted to understand what was meant
without being told at greater length that Adam had failed to
overcome Satanic strength, and all the world, and mass of sinful flesh; that Satanic strength, and all the world, and mass of
sinful flesh each describe individual trials Christ is to encounter;
or that Satanic strength, and all the world, and mass of sinful
flesh account between them for all the ills that beset mankind.
Similarly, the devil does not inform his followers pointblank
that he intends to use on Christ exactly the same methods he
had used on Adam: he simply remarks that "the way found
prosperous once / Induces best to hope of like success,"[42] goes
to the wilderness, completes the first temptation, and comes
back with the news that he finds:

> Far other labour to be undergon
> Then when I dealt with *Adam* first of men. . . .
> Therefore I am return'd, lest confidence
> Of my success with *Eve* in Paradise
> Deceive ye to perswasion over-sure
> Of like succeeding here.[43]

Again, however, the reader familiar with the triple equation
could hardly avoid concluding that these passages were based
on, and written in support of, the old Protestant contention
that Satan first tried to win Christ through doubt and distrust,

[40] *P. R.*, 1. 320-56.   [42] *P. R.*, 1. 104-5.
[41] *P. R.*, 1. 154-55; 161-62.   [43] *P. R.*, 2. 132-43.

because that was how he had first won Adam. And that the
reader would have been right in making such an assumption is
supported by the fact that Milton elsewhere declares that Satan
had won Adam through doubt and distrust: in the *Christian
Doctrine,* where the Fall is attributed in part to "incredulitate
in Deum,"[44] and in *Paradise Lost,* where the serpent persuades
Eve to eat by asking:

> Why then was this forbid? Why but to awe,
> Why but to keep ye low and ignorant,
> His worshippers?[45]

—a question which reads like a paraphrase of Andrewes' earlier
statement that in "Adam the devil first brought him to a conceit that God envied his good, and of purpose kept him hoodwinked lest he should see his good, as we see falconers put hoods
over hawks' eyes, to make them more quiet and ruly."

But if Milton followed the Protestants so far, he almost certainly followed them one step further, associated the *cibus ligni
vetitus* with Adam's *avaritia,* and therefore felt entitled to treat
the pleasures of the flesh under the heading of the "kingdoms,"
as Bale and Fletcher had before him. The second temptation,
like the first, is not *specifically* equated with a corresponding
temptation in Eden: it is merely said to be an "attempt bolder
than that on *Eve,* / And more blasphemous."[46] Like the first,
however, it was apparently written in conformity with the
traditional Protestant version of the triple equation, because
Milton places, among the attractions of Rome, earthly splendors which are also potential sources of direct physical pleasures.
When Satan concludes his description of the glories of the city,
Christ replies:

> Nor doth this grandeur and majestic show
> Of luxury, though call'd magnificence,
> More then of arms before, allure mine eye,
> Much less my mind; though thou should'st add to tell
> Thir sumptuous gluttonies, and gorgeous feasts
> On *Cittron* tables or *Atlantic* stone;
> (For I have also heard, perhaps have read)
> Thir wines of *Setia, Cales,* and *Falerne,*

---

[44] J. Milton, *Works,* 15.180-81.   [45] *P. L.,* 9.703-5.
[46] *P. R.,* 4.180-81. There is an allusion to the *cibus ligni vetitus* in 2.348-49;
but this belongs to the banqueting scene, and will be discussed in Chapter VI.

Chios and *Creet*, and how they quaff in Gold,
Crystal and Myrrhine cups imboss'd with Gems
And studs of Pearl, to me should'st tell who thirst
And hunger still.[47]

This passage in position and function corresponds very closely to Bale's description of the "meates" and Fletcher's account of the drinking-party. The other pleasure of the flesh they mention—lechery—is not actually offered to Jesus in *Paradise Regained*; but the advice Belial gives his leader at the council of demons ("Set women in his eye and in his walk")[48] makes it clear that lust could have and would have formed part of the following temptation if Satan had not rejected the suggestion because he thought it so unlikely to succeed.

The rest of the splendors which Satan offers Christ are also all, except one, universally approved by the tradition. Milton, like most Renaissance authorities,[49] belongs to the "literal" school — that is, the school which made a definite distinction between the "kingdoms" and the "glories," and believed the possession of the latter to be contingent upon the possession of the former. Milton's Satan, unlike Bale's, does not fling at Christ a heterogeneous collection of countries, followed by an equally heterogeneous array of "glories"; but that Milton's basic conception of the event was similar to Bale's is shown by the care he takes to associate each glory in its turn with the acquisition or enjoyment of actual royalty. Thus, the devil first offers Christ great riches—to enable him to become a king; then popular acclaim — to result from his assumption of the Jewish throne; then armed might — to be won by his taking command of Parthia; then earthly luxury and magnificence— to be achieved by his making himself emperor of Rome. Even the final lures — wisdom and eloquence — are described as the attributes of a real city, Athens, and held out as a means of attaining absolute power:

These here revolve, or, as thou lik'st, at home,
Till time mature thee to a Kingdom's waight:
These rules will render thee a King compleat
Within thyself, much more with Empire joyn'd,[50]

---

[47] *P. R.*, 4. 110-21.   [48] *P. R.*, 2. 154.
[49] Fletcher is the only writer I know of who treats the kingdoms allegorically.
[50] *P. R.*, 4. 280-84.

a suggestion which Christ counters by retorting that in the writings of the Hebrew prophets

> is plainest taught, and easiest learnt,
> What makes a Nation happy, and keeps it so,
> What ruins Kingdoms, and lays Cities flat;
> These only with our Law best form a King.[51]

Milton, to the best of my knowledge, is the first writer to place learning among the glories of the world—perhaps because he felt that as an honest man he could not exclude the one form of worldly activity which appealed to him most, and which he knew by personal experience to be the last infirmity of the noble mind. As Gilbert points out, however, we should note that the glory of Athens is not offered as one of the gifts of Satan, or as one of the kingdoms which he can personally bestow on Christ.[52] He presents his bargain—*Hic omnia tibi dabo, si cadens adoraveris me*—at the conclusion of the temptation of Rome. Thoroughly as Milton castigates classical philosophy and literature, he does not suggest that they are under the direct control of the devil. Wealth, glory, might, and empire are all that actually lie within his power.

The section devoted to "glory," however, is handled in a rather peculiar fashion. Since Milton is following the Luke order, he should logically use the Luke equation, making the *regna omnia mundi* the temptation of the world, and the *mitte te deorsum* the temptation of the devil. But in *Paradise Regained* the sin of Satan is specifically associated with the *regna omnia mundi*. Having failed to persuade Christ "to seek wealth / For Empire's sake," he goes on to persuade him "Empire to affect / For glory's sake."[53] Christ retorts that all common glory is false glory, and all common conquerors men

> who leave behind
> Nothing but ruin whereso'er they rove,
> And all the flourishing works of peace destroy,
> Then swell with pride, and must be titl'd Gods,
> Great Benefactors of mankind, Deliverers,
> Worship't with Temple, Priest, and Sacrifice.[54]

Satan counters this by asserting that glory must be good, since God Himself desires and exacts it of all created beings;

---

[51] *P. R.*, 4. 361-64.　　[52] Gilbert, p. 606.　　[53] *P. R.*, 3. 44-46.　　[54] *P. R.*, 3. 78-83.

and Christ parries the attack by pointing out that God alone
deserves it, not man,

> who of his own
> Hath nothing, and to whom nothing belongs
> But condemnation, ignominy, and shame.
> Who for so many benefits receiv'd
> Turn'd recreant to God, ingrate and false,
> And so of all true good himself despoil'd,
> Yet, sacrilegious, to himself would take
> That which to God alone of right belongs.[55]

And at this reply,

> Satan had not to answer, but stood struck
> With guilt of his own sin, for he himself
> Insatiable of glory had lost all.[56]

A seventeenth-century reader well grounded in the tradition
would have found this passage an exceptionally odd one. Of
course, the *regna omnia mundi* was frequently described as the
temptation of the devil, and occasionally equated with the full
text from Genesis — "And ye shall be as gods, knowing good
and evil" — even in the Renaissance.[57] The *eritis sicut dii*
was, however, much more often regarded as the parallel of
the *mitte te deorsum*. Again, the trend of seventeenth-century
opinion was to preserve the Luke equation even at the cost of
superimposing it on the order in Matthew; and for a poet
actually working with the Luke order to identify the sin of
Satan with the *regna omnia mundi* was certainly very much
out of the ordinary. Furthermore, that sin is identified not
with the whole temptation, but instead with one particular
part of it — and that part is specifically concerned with the
great man's tendency to become vainglorious to the point of
committing acts of insane presumption and behaving as if he
were equal to God. But vainglorious presumption is the very
offence which any orthodox theologian always ascribed to the

---

[55] *P. R.*, 3. 134-41.   [56] *P. R.*, 3. 146-48.
[57] Cf. Bucer's comment, above, p. 59 (note 21). Christ's condemnation of " man "
for turning recreant to God and yet sacrilegiously demanding "that which to God
alone of right belongs," suggests that Milton was thinking of this particular verse.
In *The Christian Doctrine*, he lists among the crimes of Adam and Eve " invasion
of the rights of others," " sacrilege," and " presumption in aspiring to divine attributes " — (*Works*, 15. 183).

temptation of the tower,[58] which in its turn was usually associated with the *eritis sicut dii* under any form of the triple equation, and under that of Luke, with the sin of the devil as well. What the whole passage in *Paradise Regained* most resembles, in fact, is simply the *mitte te deorsum* temptation from an ordinary Luke equation, lifted out of its proper context, embodied in a new episode, and provided with another setting. Theoretically, at least, there could be no objection to Milton's thus making vainglorious presumption a form of worldly ambition: the temptations of the world and the devil were already interchangeable; the *eritis sicut dii* might be equated with either; and things equal to the same thing surely ought to be equal to each other. But what, the seventeenth-century reader must have wondered, did Milton think he was going to make of the *mitte te deorsum* itself, when the special offence it illustrated had already been placed among the *gloriae mundi*, ascribed to Satan, and rejected by Christ?

[58] It is interesting to compare the treatment of " glory " in *Paradise Regained* with a comment on the pinnacle in Trapp's 1656 discussion of the *mitte te deorsum:* " Height of place giveth opportunity of temptation. The longest robe contracts the greatest soil: neither are any in so great danger, as those that walk on the tops of pinnacles. Even heigth it self makes mens brains to swim: As in *Diocletian,* who not content to be Emperour, would needs be adored as a god: and *Caligula,* of whom it is said, *That there was never any better servant than he, nor worse Lord.*" — p. 65.

CHAPTER VI

THE BANQUETING SCENE

The banqueting scene in *Paradise Regained* has long been a center of scholarly controversy. Brooke and Miller think it a repetition of the temptation of bread.[1] T. H. Banks regards it as a link between the temptation of bread and the temptation of the kingdoms, because it is partly concerned with the "hunger" of the one, and partly with the "glory" of the other.[2] A. H. Gilbert argues that it belongs entirely to the temptation of the kingdoms, because it occurs on the same day, is the first and lowest form of worldly splendor, and cannot be appropriately associated with the simple temptation of bread.[3]

Gilbert's theory is the only one which is backed by the tradition and in harmony with the conventional Protestant version of the triple equation. At first glance, his hypothesis seems to explain, quite clearly and acceptably, the existence and precise status of the banqueting scene: it is, as he supposed, one of the glories of the world, and corresponds exactly to the "meates" in *The Temptation of Our Lord* and the drinking-party in *Christ's Victory and Triumph*. The exclamation that interrupts the description of the banquet itself:

> Alas, how simple to these cates compared,
> Was that crude apple that diverted *Eve*![4]

is certainly an allusion to the *cibus ligni vetitus*, and can easily be construed as evidence that the scene belongs to the temptation of the kingdoms, of which the *cibus ligni vetitus* was, in Protestant doctrine, the exact counterpart.

Unfortunately, however, the manner in which Milton depicts the temptation of the kingdoms as a whole makes one doubt if this straightforward solution of the problem is altogether the right one. If the banqueting scene is really part of the tempta-

---

[1] Stopford Brooke, *Milton* (London, 1879), p. 152; Miller, p. 407.
[2] T. H. Banks, "The Banquet Scene in *Paradise Regained*," *PMLA* 45 (1940). 773-76.
[3] Gilbert, pp. 603-4.   [4] *P. R.*, 2. 348-49.

tion of the kingdoms, it ought logically to conform to the same
pattern as the other glories of the world. But this is by no
means the case. The feast is not associated with any particular
realm, nor is it in any way related to the winning or exercise
of purely human and temporal sovereignty, like the other
glories of the world. In an allegorical account of the temptation
like Pseudo-Jerome's or Fletcher's, this would not be remarkable; but in a literal account like Milton's, it is so entirely
improper that it is in itself enough to arouse suspicion.

This suspicion is further heightened when we remember that
Milton was to include among the splendors of Rome "sumptuous gluttonies and gorgeous feasts"[5] that correspond exactly
to the *cibus ligni vetitus* of the Protestant tradition. These are
certainly earthly glories which are also direct sources of physical pleasure. They clearly and unequivocally form part of the
temptation of the kingdoms; they function precisely as do the
meats of Bale and the drinking-bout of Fletcher; and they are
placed where they most logically belong—in the section specifically devoted to the seductions of luxury and magnificence.

In order to concur with Gilbert's reading of the banqueting
scene, then, we are forced to assume that Milton was guilty
not only of flagrantly repeating his effects, but of abandoning,
momentarily and for no good reason, the particular conception
of the kingdoms temptation to which he had committed himself. Neither supposition is actually untenable, but both are so
implausible that any theory which necessitates them can be acceptable only in the absence of any other adequate explanation.

Fortunately, however, it *is* possible to account for the inclu-
sion of the banqueting scene in a different manner. The longer
one studies the Protestant-Catholic controversy about the *cibus
ligni vetitus*, the more clearly one sees that all it really amounts
to is a dispute over the interpretation of motive. Did Eve want
the apple primarily as a beautiful object, a rare luxury, a glory
of the world which chanced to be a pleasure of the flesh as well?
Or did she want it primarily as a means of satisfying her appetite, and value its richness and delicacy only insofar as they
pandered to that appetite? Was she, in other words, guilty of
the sin of covetousness, or the sin of greed? Milton, apparently,

believed she was guilty of both. In *Paradise Lost*, she begins
by craving the apple simply because it is so glorious:

> Fixt on the Fruit she gaz'd, which to behold
> Might tempt alone.[6]

But then:

> the hour of Noon drew on, and wak'd
> An eager appetite, rais'd by the smell
> So savorie of that Fruit, which with desire,
> Inclinable now grown to touch or taste,
> Solicited her longing eye.[7]

She therefore ends by taking the apple not only because it is a
splendor which happens to be edible, but because it is an edible
which happens to be splendid. And judging by the amount of
space Milton devotes to the latter temptation, he evidently
thought it the more significant of the two. The motif recurs
in Eve's dream, where the false angel

> Even to my mouth of that same fruit held part
> Which he had pluckt; the pleasant savourie smell
> So quick'nd appetite, that I, methought,
> Could not but taste.[8]

The pretended serpent dwells on the same theme in his account
of his experience; he tells Eve that

> To satisfie the sharp desire I had
> Of tasting those fair Apples, I resolv'd
> Not to defer; hunger and thirst at once,
> Powerful perswaders, quick'nd at the scent
> Of that alluring Fruit, urg'd me so keene.[9]

Finally, when Michael shows Adam the vision of the sick at
the end of the epic, he explains that they suffer because

> Thir Makers Image . . . then
> Forsook them, when themselves they villifi'd
> To serve ungovern'd appetite, and took
> His image whom they serv'd, a brutish vice,
> Inductive mainly to the sin of Eve,[10]

and adds that peaceful death comes only

[6] *P. L.*, 9. 735-36.
[7] *P. L.*, 9. 739-43.
[8] *P. L.*, 5. 83-86.
[9] *P. L.*, 9. 578-88.
[10] *P. L.*, 11. 515-24.

> if thou well observe
> The rule of not too much, by temperance taught
> In what thou eatst and drinkst, seeking from thence
> Due nourishment, not gluttonous delight.[11]

It is not unreasonable to assume that Milton must have found this particular conception of the *cibus ligni vetitus* somewhat embarrassing when he began to face the problems of *Paradise Regained*. Since he was willing to admit that the apple was (to a certain extent) an earthly splendor, he could have no objection to falling in with Bale and Fletcher and treating sumptuous gluttonies and gorgeous feasts under the heading of the "kingdoms." But he was both too honest and too acute to suppose that they provided Christ with a temptation equivalent to that of Eve, as he had depicted it in his former work. Matthew and Luke had both clearly stated that the temptation of the kingdoms was the temptation of the glories of the world. The sumptuous gluttonies and gorgeous feasts belonged to that temptation only insofar as they could be described as glories of the world. It follows that Christ would have accepted them, if at all, because they *were* glories of the world—that is, as he himself points out, because he was "allured" by "this grandeur and majestic show / Of luxury, though call'd magnificence." The fact that he was hungry may have served to reinforce the appeal of the splendors; but the very nature of the trial made it impossible that appetite should have been the actual, moving, decisive consideration which brought about his surrender. That, indeed, had always been the principal defect of the Protestant equation: its inability to deal with the chief sins of the flesh except by indirection, makeshift, and ambiguity.

Milton therefore had his choice either of leaving without adequate parallel a substantial and, in his eyes, an important part of Eve's experience, or of finding some other situation he could use to show that Jesus was offered and declined an opportunity to commit the same sin she had. But he must have discovered, like Bunyan's Christian, that he was neither willing to do the first, nor able to do the second. The only other episode in Matthew or Luke susceptible of any such interpre-

---

[11] *P. L.*, 11. 530-33. Milton also states that gluttony was one of the sins which Eve committed in *The Christian Doctrine* (*Works*, 15. 180-81).

tation was the *dic ut lapides*; and the Protestant theologians, whose view of the event Milton had accepted, were firmly and even savagely convinced that the *dic ut lapides* related only to the sin of doubt and distrust, and had nothing whatever to do with the sin of appetite. Milton was not, however, an exegete or a homilist, under that immediate tyranny of the text which necessitated attaching the unlawful delights of the flesh to the *regna omnia mundi*, if they were to be introduced at all: a poet might create an independent episode of his own which answered his requirements. As we have already seen, the theory that there had been many unrecorded temptations gave him a certain amount of authority for including an incident not specifically based on any described in the Gospels [12] — though one fears he would have acted in precisely the same manner if he had had no authority but that of the Muse who inspired him ("and she was God's Holy Spirit").

The banqueting scene itself certainly has all the characteristics of an episode especially devised to cover that aspect of the *cibus ligni vetitus* which could not receive satisfactory treatment under the temptation of the kingdoms. In both cases the concrete object offered to Christ is the same — a feast of extraordinary luxury and magnificence. But in the temptation of the kingdoms, the primary and what may be called the *operative* appeal is made to the desire for glory and opulence: food served on citron tables or Atlantic stone, drink in gold, crystal, or myrrhine cups embossed with gems and studs of pearl. That Christ "thirsts and hungers still" is a secondary consideration used simply to back up the first. In the banqueting scene, on the other hand, the situation is exactly reversed; the primary and operative appeal is made to the desire for food, and the splendors that accompany it seem designed merely to excaberate appetite and render it intolerable. The ostentatious tables and highly decorated cups of Rome do not touch all the physical senses to the quick, or string each to the highest possible pitch of self-consciousness, longing, and delight, as the nymphs, the music, and the perfumed winds which appear with the banquet do. The delicacies themselves (unlike the sumptuous gluttonies and gorgeous feasts) are de-

[12] See Chapter I, p. 6.

scribed at length and depend for their effect very largely on
the purely sensory attractions of smell or taste:

> meats of noblest sort
> And savour, Beasts of chase, or Fowl of game,
> In pastry built, or from the spit, or boyl'd,
> Gris-amber-steamed; all Fish from Sea or Shore,
> Freshet or purling Brook, of shell or fin,
> And exquisitest name, for which was drain'd
> *Pontus* or *Lucrine* Bay, and Afric Coast.
> Alas how simple, to these cates compar'd,
> Was that crude Apple that diverted *Eve*!
> And at a stately side-board by the wine
> That fragrant smell diffus'd, in order stood
> Tall stripling youths.[13]

Moreover, the passage not only links the feast specifically with
the *cibus ligni vetitus*, but is curiously reminiscent of the lines
which describe Eve yielding to pure gluttony and longing for
the apple because "the pleasant savourie smell" so quickened
her appetite. The similarity between the two is all the more
significant if we remember that for a man long blind, the sensuous enjoyment of food simply as food comes entirely from its
taste and odor — and its power to attract especially from its
odor. If he had to describe a temptation of gluttony, we would
expect to find it almost inevitably centering on the "pleasant
savourie smell" which in his own experience constituted the
one physical appeal of any dish he had not yet touched.

There was, however, one serious difference between the situation of Eve and that of Christ. Eve had no justification whatever for her self-indulgence. While she may have been hungry,
she did not really need the fruit: the garden was full of food
she was entitled to take if she wished. Her eating of the apple,
therefore, could not be excused on the grounds of legitimate
compliance with what Milton called "the lawful demands of
Nature," and so might properly be ascribed to the illegitimate
and gluttonous pampering of an appetite she had other means
of satisfying. But the argument that Christ's acceptance of
the banquet would have involved a similar sin was open to the
objection Calvin had already brought against the Fathers'
interpretation of the *dic ut lapides*: "ridiculum est ad gulae

intemperium referre siquis famelicus cibum appetit quo naturae satisfaciat." [14] Since Christ, unlike Eve, was alone in a wilderness and cut off from every normal source of supply, how could one assume that the breaking of his fast would result from intemperance, and not from a proper and harmless desire for the necessary sustenance to which he had a right?

Milton meets this difficulty by making use of the same theory the Reformers had originally advanced to explain the *quadraginta dies*. As Christ puts it in the soliloquy on his hunger:

> Four times ten days I have pass'd
> Wandring this woody maze, and humane food
> Nor tasted, nor had appetite; that Fast
> To Vertue I impute not, or count part
> Of what I suffer here; if Nature need not,
> Or God support Nature without repast
> Though needing, what praise is it to endure?
> But now I feel I hunger, which declares,
> Nature hath need of what she asks; yet God
> Can satisfie that need some other way,
> Though hunger still remain: so it remain
> Without this bodies wasting, I content me,
> And from the sting of famine fear no harm,
> Nor mind it, fed with better thoughts that feed
> Mee hungring more to do my Fathers will.[15]

In other words, Christ asserts that his abstinence so far reflects no credit on him, because he has been throughout the forty days so sustained by the power of God that he did not even feel the want of food. Now, however, he has begun to hunger, "which declares / Nature hath need of what she asks;" yet, since his body is not wasted or his physical faculties impaired, he concludes that the power is still sustaining him to the extent of miraculously satisfying the *essential* demands of the flesh, and therefore feels he can afford to disregard his appetite. This leaves him in a position similar to Eve's: he longs for food, but does not actually require it. The point is made again for good measure during the conversation with the devil that directly precedes the offer of the banquet itself: Satan reminds the Lord that Hagar, Elijah, and the Children of Israel had all been fed in the wilderness, and Christ retorts:

---

[14] Calvin, *Commentarii*, p. 51.   [15] *P. R.*, 2. 245-59.

What conclud'st thou hence?
They all had need, I as thou seest have none.[16]

It follows that, in yielding to his hunger for the banquet, Christ would have committed the same sin Eve committed by yielding to *her* hunger for the *cibus ligni vetitus*: the sin of taking food he did not really need because its flavor, delicacy, and immediate appeal proved too much for a greed he should have been able to control. Since he was no longer so supported by divine strength that he felt no appetite whatever, his refusal constituted a legitimate act of virtue, as meritorious as Eve's consent under similar circumstances had been wicked. The parallel between the temptation in *Paradise Lost* and the one in *Paradise Regained* was thus complete.

Satan, of course, is much too subtle to urge Christ straightforwardly to eat, drink, and be merry because the occasion gives him such an excellent opportunity to indulge in gluttony. He does not even dwell on the deliciousness and sensuous attractions of the banquet; but presenting it, according to plan, as "that which only seems to satisfy / Lawful desires of nature, not beyond,"[17] he argues merely that Christ is hungry and ought to have food because as the Son of God he has a right to any created thing in the world that might serve or help him. The banquet itself, he asserts, is not even his own gift, but a little tribute from the powers of Nature, which are anxious to minister to Christ and acknowledge him as their lawful Lord. In other words, Satan is back at the old game of combining temptation with an effort to make Jesus admit or claim his divinity, as he would tacitly do if he accepted the offering after it had been defined in those particular terms.

Christ, however, does not simply turn on the devil and call him a liar whose real purpose is to seduce him into committing a sin of the flesh. He is content instead to meet Satan on his own ground and demolish his case even as he chooses to present it:

Said'st thou not that to all things I had right?
And who withholds my power that right to use?
Shall I receive by gift what of my own,
When and where likes me best, I can command?

---

[16] *P. R.*, 2. 318-19.   [17] *P. R.*, 2. 229-30.

> I can at will, doubt not, as soon as thou,
> Command a table in this wilderness,
> And call swift flights of angels ministrant,
> Array'd in glory on my cup to attend.
> Why shouldst thou then obtrude this diligence
> In vain, where no acceptance it can find?
> And with my hunger what hast thou to do?
> Thy pompous delicacies I contemn,
> And count thy specious gifts no gifts but guiles.[18]

This is to say in effect: If I *am* the Son of God, as you say that I am, with power over the resources of the world, then why should you trouble yourself to see my needs satisfied, when according to your own argument, I can have whatever I like merely by ordering it? The declaration of Christ's rank is evidently meant to be entirely hypothetical: the one positive statement he makes is covered by the rush of questions which precede and follow it, nor does Satan take it as the proof or affirmation which he is trying to obtain. As usual, the Lord has neither denied nor acknowledged his real identity: he has merely put the whole question aside without committing himself.

A modern reader unfamiliar with the tradition might well be puzzled by this interchange of arguments, and even wonder if Satan's whole aim in offering the banquet is not to persuade Christ to admit his Godhead by accepting it, since this is the one issue which is fought out at any length. On the other hand, the luxury and profusion of the scene suggest that he is intended to regard it as part of the temptation of the kingdoms, one of the glories of the world. To add to his confusion, he sees the feast's obvious appeal to Christ's appetite, but hardly knows what to make of it, because he naturally thinks of the *dic ut lapides* as the temptation of hunger and therefore hesitates to credit Milton with what seems like mere unintelligent repetition. Confronted by so many possibilities, and with no real evidence as to which is intended to be the real main-spring of the episode, he ends in a state of uncertainty and controversy very unlikely to have troubled the seventeenth-century reader. That reader had been brought up on the belief that the devil's first purpose was to persuade Christ actually to *sin*—if possible, to sin in such a way as to reveal his true identity, but at any

[18] *P. R.*, 2. 379-91.

event, to sin. His knowledge of the triple equation, in conjunction with Milton's presentation of the whole incident, would be quite enough to show him which particular sin Satan meant the Lord to commit. Once the question of Satan's primary object was settled, the rest of the scene would immediately fall into line — the luxuries become simply the proper vehicle for a temptation of sensuality, and the debate over the Lord's identity simply an intellectual skirmish in which Christ defeats the devil on a point of logic—very satisfying to a Puritan dialectician, but not to be confused with the main issue. And as if to insure that there should be no doubt as to what that main issue was, Milton states it clearly at the end of the scene, when Satan, having failed, ruefully sums up the situation, and for the first time truthfully admits his real purpose:

> By hunger, that each other creature tames,
> Thou art not to be harm'd, therefore not mov'd;
> Thy temperance invincible besides,
> For no allurement yields to appetite.[19]

It is impossible to say whether the composition of the banqueting scene was in any way influenced by a conscious approval of the Fathers, or a conscious determination to get back to that direct and unequivocal temptation of the flesh which makes their version of the triple equation so satisfactory. But the fact remains that the episode as it stands can be fairly described as the Protestant equivalent of the old *gula* temptation of medieval theology, purged of those elements which made it so objectionable as long as it was identified with the *dic ut lapides* and so unsatisfactory as long as it was merely attached, in a subordinate and ambiguous form, to the *regna omnia mundi*. What effect it would have on Milton's final version of the triple equation cannot be decided until we have all the possible factors of that equation in our hands.

[19] *P. R.*, 2. 406-9.

Chapter VII

THE TEMPTATION OF THE TOWER

The temptation of the tower provoked no such controversy between Catholic and Protestant theologians as had the *quadraginta dies* and the temptation of bread; indeed, during the Renaissance, the great majority in both camps continued to accept views of the event which carry on or develop, rather than break with, those current in the Middle Ages. The essential point of their doctrine has already been dealt with: the belief that Christ was urged to commit the sin of vainglorious presumption, corresponding in the triple equation to Adam's desire to be as God and to all men's inclination to "swell and thinke highly of themselves for some grace they haue receiued, of learning, wit, eloquence. &c."[1] Thus, when Satan took Christ (whether bodily or by means of a vision) to the summit of the Temple, he pressed him, as Udall paraphrases the text,

as if he should have said, if thou be certaine that thou art the verie sonne of God, of such Maiestie and power: it is meete and convenient, that thou make it knowne unto the world, by some notable & singuler miracle, that they may have occasion to give thee that honour, which is due to such a person: for which there is no more fit way, then now that thou art here aloft, uppon the top of the temple . . . to throw thy selfe downe, from hence headlong unto the ground, which when the men of Jerusalem do behold, they cannot choose but confesse thee to be the onely, and very sonne of the everlasting God, and receive thee with a common applause, to be their Saviour and redeemer, and so advaunce thee among them unto great honour.[2]

In making this proposal, however, Satan really would "have had our Saviour to haue done it out of presumption and vaineglory."[3] The sin of vain glory lay in his "desiring by this

---

[1] Perkins, p. 68. St. Bruno Astensius (cols. 92-93) and Jeremy Taylor (p. 151) also point out that the height of the pinnacle symbolizes the situation of those whose elevated worldly position makes them most susceptible to vainglory, in particular the great men of the Church, to whom the phrase "set upon the pinnacle of the Temple" is in its metaphorical sense especially appropriate. Cf. Trapp's note, above, Chapter V, p. 69.

[2] Udall, sig. E7ʳ–E7ᵛ.

[3] Dyke, p. 283. See also Ward, pp. 102-3; Perkins, p. 65; Cradock, p. 40; I. H., p. 271.

80

meanes to be accounted of all the Sonne of God,"[4] a theory
which Ward and the authors of the *Assembly's Annotations*
support by the argument that otherwise the trial need not
have taken place in a crowded city, where an audience would
be on hand to applaud the miracle: "the devil," as the *Assembly's Annotations* put it, "might have set him on some rock
in the wilderness: but he thought Jesus would be more willing
to shew himself at Jerusalem, and from the Temple."[5] The sin
of presumption, on the other hand, lay in Christ's trusting to
"Gods power and promise for preservation without warrant,"[6]
or, to put it differently, in his recklessly flinging himself into
needless danger to prove that the angels would rescue him.
The great majority of exegetes reasoned that Christ's reply—
"It is written again, Thou shalt not tempt the Lord thy God"
—ought to be interpreted as: "Thou shalt not make trial of
the Lord thy God," for "we are said to tempt God, when we
make an unnecessary experiment of his Truth, Goodness, and
Power and Care of us, having had sufficient assurance of these
things before."[7] Or, as Xavier has it,

respondit, Rursus scriptum est, Dominum tuum Deum ne tenta:
Id est, bonum est spem habere, Deum in periculis & aerumnis adju-
torem nostrum futurum. veruntamen non vult ut propter istem
spem nos ipsos sine causa in id quod perdere posset conjiciamus.[8]

To back this interpretation of the text, there was the fact that
Christ's reply is simply a quotation of Deuteronomy 6:16 —
"ye shall not tempt the Lord your God, as ye tempted him
at Massah" — where the expression "tempt" certainly means
"make trial" and refers to the occasion when the Jews of the

[4] Dyke, p. 284.
[5] *Assembly's Annotations* 2. sig. A4ʳ. See also Ward, p. 102. St. Thomas Aquinas
(*Summa Theologica*, pars 3, quaest. 41, art. 4) suggests that Jesus avoided any
possible publicity by making himself invisible!
[6] Dyke, p. 284.
[7] Manton, p. 91.
[8] Xavier, p. 129. See also Euthymius Zigabenus, col. 178; Rupertus Abbas, col.
1548; Rabanus Maurus, *In Matthaeum*, col. 783; Calvin, *Commentarii*, p. 53; Bale,
sig. D3ᵛ; Marlorate, p. 64; Luca, col. 545; T. Taylor, pp. 269-78; J. Taylor, pp. 143-
44; Jansen, col. 546; *Assembly's Annotations*, 2. sig. A4ʳ; Piscator, p. 59; Bucer,
fol. 99ᵛ; Dyke, p. 311; Ward, p. 108; Perkins, p. 79; Leigh, p. 9; Lapide, p. 105;
Downame, p. 93; Chemnitius, pp. 45-47.

Exodus insisted upon having a sign from Heaven to prove whether the Lord was with them or not.[9]

Exegetes of a logical turn of mind were therefore careful to point out that Christ was in no actual danger: Satan would not have thrust him down from the pinnacle, either because he had no power to force men to yield to temptation,[10] or because he would not even if he could, for if Christ fell involuntarily he would not commit a sin: "no man tempteth God which doth not willingly, without necessitie cast himself into daunger, but against his will is brought thereto."[11] Furthermore, some argued, Jesus could easily have descended from the roof in some more normal way: "poterat enim Christus ex pinnaculo templi per gradus vel funes descendere, uti descendunt fabri: non ergo necesse erat ex eo se praecipitaret."[12] It followed that if Christ had assented to the devil's suggestion, he would not have been entitled to that protection of the angels which Satan craftily promises him, because (as the tempter does *not* make clear) they only "keep thee in all thy ways,"[13] —that is, as Jeremy Taylor says, "in the ways of Nature, and while [men] are doing their duty."[14] Some of the earlier theologians—notably Chrysostom, Jerome, Theophylactus, and Origen—had preferred to argue that while the devil had indeed twisted the text, he had done so by failing to point out that the promise applied only to holy men, and not to Christ, who as God-man and master of the angels, needed no help from them.[15] By the Renaissance, however, this explanation had

---

[9] Rupertas Abbas, col. 1548. See also Euthymius Zigabenus, col. 178; Luca, col. 545; and D. Heinsius, *Sacrarum Exercitationum ad Novum Testamentum Libri XX* (Cambridge, 1640), p. 21.

[10] Blackwood, p. 97; Fuller, pp. 86-87; Cradock, p. 40; Woodhead, p. 118.

[11] Marlorate, p. 63. See also *Assembly's Annotations*, 2. sig. A4^r and sig. J5^r; Cradock, p. 40; Manton, p. 58.

[12] Lapide, p. 105. See also Wyclif, 1.110; T. Taylor, p. 218; Matthew Poole, *Annotations Upon the Holy Bible* [1680] (Edinburgh, 1801); Udall, sig. F6^v; Perkins, p. 84; I. H., p. 272; Downame, p. 93; Blackwood, p. 102; Fuller, p. 122; Manton, p. 57.

[13] Psalms 91:11: "For he shall give his angels charge over thee, to keep thee in all thy ways."

[14] J. Taylor, p. 151. See also Blackwood, p. 100; Bale, sig. D3^v; Luca, col. 543; Piscator, p. 59; Udall, sig. F6^v; Bucer, fols. 99^r–99^v; Dyke, p. 293; Mayer, p. 81; Fuller, pp. 109-10; Cradock, p. 40; Chemnitius, p. 45; Calvin, *Commentarii*, p. 53.

[15] Chrysostom, col. 686; Jerome, col. 32; Theophylactus, *Enarratio in Evangelium Matthaei*, col. 182; Origen, *In Lucam Homiliae*, col. 1882.

fallen out of favor, and was almost completely superseded by the alternative or "all-thy-ways" theory, perhaps because the latter not only made better sense in itself, but fitted more gracefully into the hypothesis that Christ was tempted to make a wholly arbitrary and unnecessary experiment of God's providence, and squared more neatly with the doctrine that he was acting *quasi homo*, under the same conditions as his humblest follower.

There were commentators, on the other hand, who held that "Thou shalt not tempt the Lord thy God," meant no more than "Thou shalt not tempt *me*": "hoc diabolo dicit, Me Dominum tuum non tentabis."[16] Those who actually support this hypothesis are all Church Fathers, but Thomas Taylor alludes to it in a manner which shows that it was still current in the seventeenth century: "Some thinke that the pronoune (*Thou*) is to be referred to Satan; and (*the Lord thy God*) to Christ himselfe, as though Christ had said, Thou shalt not tempt me."[17] But as a doctrine it never won general acceptance, probably because it ran counter to the entire trend of the tradition, with its emphasis on the humanity of Christ and the exemplary nature of his replies to the devil. Taylor gives a whole series of arguments against the theory: it was never written that Satan should not tempt Christ — if it had been, it would be false; the prohibition is a negative command of God, which binds all persons at all times and all places, and is not to be restricted to this particular occasion; Satan continues to tempt Christ, which would make the injunction meaningless if it referred to Jesus himself; Satan was irrecoverably fallen, and so though Christ was his Lord in "respect of his power," yet he was "not his God in respect of the Couenant of Grace, which those words haue speciall respect unto"; and finally, "Christ in this humble estate would not manifeste himself, much lesse call himselfe Lord and God."[18] It is hardly

---

[16] Pseudo-Chrysostom, col. 686. See also St. Hilary, *Commentarius in Matthaeum*, col. 930; Pseudo-Jerome, col. 559; Walafridus Strabus, *Expositio in Quatuor Evangelia*, col. 870. Cf. St. Ambrose, *Expositionis in Lucam*, col. 1703: "Dominus respondit ei: *Non tentabis Dominum Deum tuum.* In quo et Dominum et Deum Christum, et Patrem et Filium potestatis unius esse cognoscis, juxta quod scriptum est: 'Ego et Pater unum sumus (*Joan.*, X, 30).'" Pseudo-Chrysostom, St. Hilary, and St. Ambrose still, however, regard the temptation itself as one of presumption.

[17] T. Taylor, p. 269.   [18] *Ibid.*, p. 269.

surprising, after all this, to find that most orthodox theologians preferred the other interpretation of the text. Another point frequently debated was the exact meaning of the word "pinnacle." Many commentators did not trouble to explain it, or contented themselves with some such vague phrase as "in templi summo," [19] or "in sublimi posito." [20] But others attempted more specific definitions, especially during the Renaissance, when conflicting opinions on the question became as plentiful as blackberries. One group held that the word merely signified the flat roof which was to be expected in an Eastern building:

Pinnaculum autem summitas est tecti. Non enim habebat templum culmen in superioribus sicut nec tabernaculum, sed erat aequale, quomodo omnibus in Palaestina et Ægypto domus aedificantibus facere moris est. [21]

But since the word "pinnacle" was derived from the Greek πτερύγιον, "diminutium ab ala," [22] many Renaissance theologians felt that it ought to refer to a part of the building which bore some actual architectural resemblance to a "little wing." Some, therefore, argued that while the roof was indeed flat, it was surrounded by a battlement or balaustrade to prevent accidents, as the Law of Moses ordained that all such roofs should be, [23] and that this railing was itself the "pinnacle" on which Satan placed Christ: "so an uprising border was named, which like a leaning or rail was made round the flat covering of the Temple; to hinder anyone from falling off easily." [24]

[19] St. Hilary, *Commentarius in Matthaeum*, col. 929.

[20] Pseudo-Chrysostom, col. 685.

[21] Rabanus Maurus, *In Matthaeum*, col. 782; Bede, *In Matthaei Evangelium Expositio*, col. 19. See also Diodate (sec. sig. C3r), who suggests that the temptation may have taken place "upon the roof of the porch of the Temple, sixty cubits high, *Ezra* 6. 3 "; Luca (col. 542), who agrees, adding that the place was especially appropriate, since it overlooked a courtyard thronged with worshippers; Cradock (p. 40): "He sets him upon a *Pinacle* or *Turret* of the temple." A window in Chartres Cathedral, a woodcut in the *Bibel Froschzauer* (p. clxxxviiiv, sig. Zz8v), and another in the Kitto Bible show Christ and Satan standing together on a flat roof.

[22] Erasmus, *Novum Instrumentum cum Annotationes*, p. 244. See also *Dutch Annotations*, 2. sig. Cv; Maldonatus, cols. 89-90; Lapide, p. 104; Chemnitius, p. 44.

[23] Deuteronomy 22:8.

[24] *Dutch Annotations*, 2. sig. Cv. See also Henry Hammond, p. 20; Piscator, p. 50; Perkins, p. 64; Maldonatus, cols. 89-90; Fuller, p. 76; Jansen, cols. 541-42; Beza, p. 12; T. Taylor, p. 218; J. Taylor, p. 143; a woodcut in the Kitto Bible and

Since the battlement "ab aedificiis extabat, & veluti in aere pendere, ut alae similis," [25] this definition met the conditions of the derivation satisfactorily enough, and seems to have been the most popular one current in the Renaissance. Other commentators, however, maintained that the "pinnacle" was simply a "pinnacle" in the ordinary sense of the word: "the very shafte or steple, being the highest place of the temple, uppon the which commonly we set wethercockes for the wynde." [26] As evidence that the temple possessed such decorations, Fuller and Chemnitius quote Josephus as authority that the roof was topped with golden spires, which, as Fuller puts it, "were pointed sharp as a needle, purposely to prevent birds sitting and defiling upon them." [27] Still other exegetes defined the pinnacle as a peaked gable; [28] as one of the high "polished corners" at the top of the temple; [29] as a sort of gutter or "cornice jetting out" from the flat roof — as "well for ornament as to convey away the rain water"; [30] or, in a brave effort to combine as many theories as possible, as one of the spires which adorned the broad balaustrade which in turn surrounded the flat roof of the temple. [31]

The possibility that the temptation might have taken place on a pointed roof, a sharp spire, or a projecting cornice naturally raised the question: how was Christ able to stand on it without falling involuntarily, which would have nullified the

---

a print by Jerome Wierix, after Bernardino Passeri, which show Christ and Satan standing together on the edge of the balaustrade.

[25] Maldonatus, cols. 89-90.

[26] Marlorate, p. 60; Woodhead, p. 117. Chemnitius (p. 44) gives this explanation as a possible alternative to his own; Fuller (p. 76) and Maldonatus (col. 89) and Perkins (p. 64) list but reject it.

[27] Fuller, p. 76. Chemnitius, p. 44: "Et extat locus de templo apud Iosephum de bello Iudaico lib. 6. cap. 6. In summo aureis verubus horrebat accutissimis, ne ab insidentibus avibus pollueretur." Cf. Perkins, p. 64: "Some think that it was a sharpe broach gilded to some especiall use."

[28] Theophylactus, col. 182; Blackwood, p. 97. Maldonatus (col. 89) considers the theory, but rejects it on the ground that "scimus neque templum neque caeteras in Palestina domus eiusmodi tecta habuisse, quin superne plane erant."

[29] Chemnitius, pp. 44-45. Perkins (p. 65) gives the theory as a possible alternative to his own.

[30] Diodate, sec. sig. C3r, as an alternative to the theory that the temptation took place on the flat roof.

[31] Manton, p. 54. See also Lapide, p. 104; and Mayer, p. 78: "the Temple was plaine upon the top, having three battlements, and upon every of these was a pinnacle, upon one of which he did set Christ."

whole temptation? Woodhead thinks that the devil "set and held him" there, Blackwood that the pinnacle "had some breadth upon it, wherein a man might stand," Lapide that either explanation may be true.[32] Bilson, arguing that Christ may have made use of his own miraculous powers to see all the kingdoms of the world in a moment of time, "which in this case he might like, lest the deuill should despise him, as hauing greater power and cleerer sight then Christ did," goes on to remark:

> For which cause also Christ would stand upon the pinnacle of the Temple without the diuels helpe, to let him know, that he wanted not power to doe greater things then the diuell urged him unto; but onely that hee would take his owne time, and doe nothing at the diuels instigation or motion, nor repugnant to the will and pleasure of God.[33]

But in view of the doctrine that Christ was undergoing the temptation as a man, and that a display of his miraculous powers was just what the devil hoped to provoke, it is hardly surprising to find that Bilson's theory received no support, and indeed, as far as I know, was never so much as mentioned by any other theologian of the tradition.

The chief result of all the argument over the word "pinnacle" was the addition of a new and subtle element to discussion of the temptation of the tower. When a commentator thought of Christ as actually standing balanced on a parapet over a dizzy height, as poised on some foothold of a steep gable, or held by Satan on the top of a spire, he was naturally likely to be much more impressed by the horror and precariousness of the Lord's position than the exegete who merely thought of the scene as taking place on a flat roof or a vague and undefined eminence of the temple. "The place," according to Thomas Taylor, "was full of danger to stand upon, and much more for the height to fall from";[34] and he is backed by Perkins: "it was a dangerous place";[35] by Dyke: "[Satan] tooke the opportunity of this place, and the danger thereof for Christ to stand long upon it, to urge his temptation";[36] by Jeremy Taylor: "there

---

[32] Woodhead, p. 118; Blackwood, p. 97; Lapide, p. 104.
[33] Bilson, p. 309.
[34] T. Taylor, p. 182.
[35] Perkins, p. 65.
[36] Dyke, p. 280.

also the station is less firm, the posture most uneasie, the prospect vertiginous ";[37] by Chemnitius: "hoc certum est, locum fuisse in summo templi fastigio, ubi sine periculo non poterat consisti ";[38] and by Fuller: "Why could not [the devil] thrust Christ down, standing now on so ticklish terms as the top of a pinacle? One shove with his shoulder, nay, one touch with his hand, might have done the deed."[39] But Fuller, Perkins, and Thomas Taylor, in order not to bring into question the essential doctrine that Christ was in no real peril save from his own vanity and presumption, carefully observe that he could still have climbed down and escaped by the stairs,[40] while all the commentators quoted, with the exception of Chemnitius, take pains to make it clear that Satan either could not or would not force Christ from the pinnacle.[41] Indeed, if they had followed through the logical implications of this theory, they might have added that even had Christ accidentally slipped, the devil would have caught him, since if he had not fallen of his own free will, the whole temptation would have been invalidated. Under these circumstances, it seems to make very little difference whether the pinnacle was dangerous or not, and perhaps that is the reason why more exegetes do not emphasize the point.

It was, of course, possible to argue that Satan hoped the very horror and precariousness of the Lord's position might have their effect on his mind—might so terrify or overwhelm him that he would lose control of himself out of sheer panic. Dyke may have been thinking of something of the sort when he remarked that the devil " tooke the opportunity of this place, and the danger thereof for Christ to stand long upon it, to urge his temptation," but the sentence is too vague to be of any great significance. Thomas Taylor writes: " This was the houre of the power of darkenes, wherein Satan was allowed to take all

---

[37] Jeremy Taylor, p. 151.   [38] Chemnitius, p. 45.   [39] Fuller, p. 86.

[40] Fuller, p. 122; Perkins, pp. 64-65; Thomas Taylor, p. 218. All three believed the pinnacle to be a low balaustrade or battlement, from which it would have been possible to get to the roof. Woodhead, who defined the pinnacle as a spire on which Satan held Christ, was obliged to concede that " from this summity, where he was placed, there were no stairs or other passable descent," but goes on to say that Satan could not throw Christ down. — p. 117.

[41] T. Taylor, pp. 212-13; Perkins, p. 65; Dyke, p. 281; J. Taylor, p. 151; Fuller, pp. 86-87.

aduantages to further his temptations: and he might thinke this violent transportation a meanes, *either* of shaking Christs faith with terror and feare of what might become of him . . . *or else* to make him swell with pride and insolencie," [42] but he presents the suggestion only as one of two possibilities and is speaking of the journey to the temple rather than the temptation itself. The one commentator who really makes the point roundly is Eliot:

> The second sort of Temptations which Jesus Christ did conflict with, & conquer is fear, which layeth Faith prostrate, and raiseth unbelief to use carnal wisdom and shifts to help our selves, and stirreth up carnal confidence and presumption in a misapplyed promise. . . . One while he was transported on to the top of one of the Pinacles of the Temple, and there was affected and terrified with fear.[43]

Eliot, however, is an extremely unconventional and independent theologian, and his theory was not one likely to find favor in the eyes of the more orthodox. In the first place, its effect was to replace the temptation of vainglorious presumption with one of panic, and thus to destroy the triple equation—for Eliot's attempt to work "carnal confidence" into his argument is a mere verbal quibble which does not meet the needs of the case at all. Furthermore, while many exegetes agreed that Satan did try to terrorize Christ, they preferred to think that he did so at a later date. Luke, though he says that the devil departed only when all the temptations were over, adds that he left merely for "a season." [44] This was easily explained by asserting that Satan can tempt either by "fraud" or by "violence": that is, either by persuasion or by fear. In the wilderness, he assailed Christ with persuasion only; afterwards, at the time of the Passion, he tried to shake him through threats of death and torture: "et tamen per illam impugnationem videbatur Christum tentare de tristia et odio proximorum." [45] True, some commentators held that Satan left Christ only to return later

[42] T. Taylor, p. 190.
[43] John Eliot, *A Harmony of the Gospels* (Boston, 1678), pp. 59-61.
[44] Luke 4:13.
[45] St. Thomas Aquinas, *Summa Theologica*, pars 3, quaest. 41, art. 3. See also Euthymius Zigabenus, col. 182; Theophylactus, *Enarratio in Evangelium Lucae*, cols. 747-48; Luca, col. 546; Andrewes, p. 494; *Assembly's Annotations*, 2. sig. J5ʳ; Diodate, sec. sig. M3ʳ; *Dutch Annotations*, 2. sig. L4ʳ.

with more temptations of the same kind as had already failed in the wilderness; [46] and this school of thought would at least not have found Eliot's theory untenable because it necessitated a form of temptation which Satan did not by definition undertake at the time. But in any event it is highly improbable that even they would have submitted to the wrecking of the triple equation and the undercutting of the ancient and honored doctrine that the temptation was one of vain glory and presumption. And therefore, natural and perhaps inevitable as it may have been for a theologian to wonder what significance the dangerousness of the pinnacle might have, the orthodox carefully refrained from following up the simplest and most obvious line of speculation, closely though a Dyke or a Taylor might skirmish about it.

Eliot's theory was not the only heterodox explanation of the episode: there was also the view that Satan did not actually tempt Christ to presume or to parade his divinity, but to commit suicide. This curious notion seems to have originated, in all innocence, with those exegetes who liked to improve an occasion by breaking off their commentary to instruct their readers on some point of morality suggested by the text under examination. For example, Marlorate, after making the conventional observation that "no man tempteth God which doth not willingly, without necessitie, cast himself into daunger, but against his will is brought thereto," remarks in passing, "Hereby it cometh . . . that [Satan] drowneth not ye desperate against their wills, he hangeth them not, he cutteth not their throates, but by his temptations he bringeth it to passe, that they do unto them selves such violence." [47] Fuller carries the matter a little further: he introduces a much longer discussion of suicide, and associates it much more directly with Christ himself: "Observe in the Text, The *Hook* . . . and The *Bait* . . . The *Hook*, in general, the sin of *Presumption*: in particular, *Self-homicide*." Or, to put it differently, Christ, out of presumption, was to act in such a manner as to end his own life. The careful wording, however, is obviously intended to keep clear the proper distinction between the motive and the event, the

[46] See for example: Lapide, p. 107; Capel, p. 51; Fuller, p. 179; Allen, p. 81.
[47] Marlorate, p. 63.

temptation and its consequences, the sin and its outcome; Fuller does not say that Christ *intended* to kill himself, or that Satan was urging him to do so, while the lengthy dissertation on suicide which follows treats the subject in general terms and has nothing to do with the temptation of the tower.[48] Christopher Blackwood apparently intended to say little more than Fuller did, but his mind was less precise and the results are less satisfactory. He busies himself chiefly with warning his readers to pay no heed to the plausible reasons that Satan will give them for making away with themselves, for he gave Christ equally plausible reasons for throwing himself down from the tower.[49] Blackwood, however, does not do enough to bring out the essential difference between Christ's temptation (to presume) and ours (to make away with ourselves) — he never says in so many words that Christ *was* tempted to presume, while the only sin he specifically warns his readers against is self-destruction, as if that were the one from which the Lord wished to protect them by the force of his example — and in his hands the distinction which Fuller had so carefully made becomes vague and confusing. But it was John Trapp who carried the heresy to its logical conclusion, and presented the *mitte te deorsum* as a true temptation of suicide:

Here our Saviour is tempted to self-murther, by an old Manslayer. And when *Moses, Elias, Jonas,* and others of the best sort of Saints were in a fit of discontent, and grew weary of their lives, wishing for death, Divines doubt not but Satan gave a push at them with his ten horns, to dispatch, and ease them of the present trouble, by cutting off their own days. A dangerous and hideous temptation; yet such as may befal the best.[50]

Curiously enough, however, Trapp apparently still dimly associated the episode with the delusions of vain glory, for when he turns to the pinnacle itself, it is to make the perfectly conventional observation that its height symbolizes the lofty social position of those who are especially likely to commit excesses of self-esteem and swollen vanity.[51] Nothing else he says would have been acceptable to any orthodox theologian, since his theory, like Eliot's, did away with the temptation of vain-

---

[48] Fuller, pp. 82 ff.
[49] Blackwood, pp. 97-102, *passim.*

[50] Trapp, p. 35.
[51] See Chapter V, p. 69.

glorious presumption and wrecked the traditional form of the triple equation. Trapp himself seems to have been somewhat concerned over the loss of the triple equation: he does not try to construct a new set of parallels between Christ and Adam, but he manages to salvage a remnant of the original by describing the *regna omnia mundi* as a combined temptation of the world, the flesh, and the devil:

Gain and glory? Rule and Riches? . . . Set but a wedge of Gold in sight, and *Joshua* (that could stay the course of the Sun) cannot stay *Achan* from lusting and laying hold on it. *Balaams* Ass never gallops fast fast enough after preferment. And *Zimri* will have his *Cozbi*, though he die for it. These three enchantresses, *The lust of the flesh, the lust of the eye, and the pride of life*; Pleasure, Profit, and Preferment (the worldly mans Trinity) whom have they not bewitched, befooled, bebeasted? [52]

As a result, Trapp could still, if challenged, have argued that Satan urged Christ to commit the three types of sin out of which all others grow. The solution was an ingenious but almost an inevitable one. Under the Protestant form of the triple equation, the temptation of the flesh was already attached, for all practical purposes, to the *regna omnia mundi*, which in their turn already represented either the temptation of the world or the temptation of the devil, and therefore why not both? — why not, in fact, all three? As long as the traditional equation dominated theology, it was most unlikely that the question would be raised; but once a writer found himself obliged to give up the traditional equation, and yet anxious to retain some form of the world-flesh-devil hypothesis, the feasibility of utilizing the *regna omnia mundi* for the purpose must have fairly leaped to the eye.

No other commentators, however, went so far as Trapp and Eliot did, and very few cared to dispute standard belief about the *mitte te deorsum* at all. Indeed, if one asks how much of the available material on the subject was likely to appeal to a learned and intelligent poet writing in the seventeenth century, the question at first glance seems delightfully easy to answer. Such a poet, as we know, frequently had his choice of more than one equally popular and acceptable interpretation of the

[52] Trapp, p. 38.

same text; there were, for instance, two schools of thought on such matters as Satan's motive in undertaking the temptation, the significance of the angels' ministry, the character of the attacks Christ suffered after he left the wilderness, and so on, with large and reputable groups backing both theories. But this is not true of the temptation of the tower. The alternate reading of the "all-thy-ways" text common in the Middle Ages had dropped out of use by the Renaissance. The version of the *non tentabis* which identified Christ as *Dominum Deum tuum* was highly questionable and could hardly have been accepted in the face of objections like those Thomas Taylor brings against it. Eliot's attempt to make the temptation one of fear was obviously a mere aberration, induced by reading too much significance into the dangers of the pinnacle. Much the same could be said of Trapp's hypothesis, clearly the result of a confused mind's misapplication of the casual remarks on suicide which more sensible commentators occasionally brought into their work. Neither theory had the slightest standing: Taylor at least felt that the *non tentabis* opinion needed refutation, whereas no exegete out of the fairly comprehensive group here considered so much as mentions the others, even to deny them; in fact, it is very unlikely that the hypothetical poet would have heard of them at all.

We might reasonably suppose, therefore, that he would hew to the established line that the temptation was one of vainglorious presumption. In Milton's case, this would be all the more likely, in view of the fact that he elsewhere describes "an overweening presumption" as one of the sins against God opposed to the "virtues belonging to the worship of God," and cites Matthew 4: 6-7, the *mitte te deorsum* with Christ's reply, as an illustrative text.[53] Furthermore, he was writing a companion-piece to *Paradise Lost*, and so would have a peculiar interest in maintaining the triple equation intact. We would naturally expect to find Satan dwelling on the triumph of gliding down under the eyes of an adoring multitude, and Christ refusing it on the grounds that he must not make unnecessary trial of his Father. And, since Milton was a very careful worker, the scene would very likely take place on a flat roof, *behind*

[53] Milton, *The Christian Doctrine*, in *Works*, 18. 54-55.

a good high parapet, so that the reader could be in no possible doubt that Christ would fall out of vainglorious presumption alone. To make the pinnacle a narrow balaustrade or, worse still, a sharp spire would merely divert his mind from the real issue and lay it open to those irrelevant suggestions of danger, panic, and terrorism which were already creeping into much Renaissance speculation and threatening to blur the clean outlines of the temptation.

But what do we actually find in *Paradise Regained?* According to Milton, Satan takes Christ back to the wilderness at the end of the second day, pretends to leave him, and then raises a dreadful storm " to tempt the Son of God with terrors dire." [54] In the morning he returns,

> Yet with no new device, they all were spent;
> Rather by this his last affront resolv'd,
> Desperate of better course, to vent his rage,
> And mad despite to be so oft repell'd.[55]

He first attempts to cow the Lord by warning him that the storm portends his future: "many a hard assay / Of dangers, and adversities and pains." [56] Then, when Christ refuses to be properly impressed by these threats and sinister forebodings, he loses all control of himself, tells his victim in so many words why he has undertaken the temptation, and confesses that he has so far failed to discover what he has come to learn:

> And opportunity I here I have had
> To try thee, sift thee, and confess have found thee
> Proof against all temptation as a rock
> Of Adamant, and a Centre, firm:
> To the utmost of meer man both wise and good,
> Not more; for Honours, Riches, Kingdoms, Glory
> Have been before contemn'd, and may again:
> Therefore to know what more thou art than man,
> Worth naming Son of God by voice from Heav'n,
> Another method I must now begin.[57]

Thereupon, he snatches Christ up and carries him to Jerusalem, where

[54] *P. R.*, 4. 431.   [56] *P. R.*, 4. 487-88.
[55] *P. R.*, 4. 443-46.   [57] *P. R.*, 4. 531-40.

               the glorious Temple rear'd
Her pile, far off appearing like a Mount
Of Alabaster, top't with golden Spires:
There on the highest Pinnacle he set
The Son of God; and added thus in scorn:
            There stand, if thou wilt stand; to stand upright
Will ask thee skill; I to thy Father's house
Have brought thee, and highest plac't, highest is best,
Now show thy Progeny; if not to stand,
Cast thyself down; safely if Son of God:
For it is written, He will give command
Concerning thee to his Angels, in thir hands
They shall up lift thee, lest at any time
Thou chance to dash thy foot against a stone.
            To whom thus Jesus: also it is written,
Tempt not the Lord thy God; he said and stood.
But Satan smitten with amazement fell . . .
And to his crew that sat consulting, brought
Joyless triumphals of his hop't success,
Ruin, and desperation, and dismay,
Who durst so proudly tempt the Son of God.[58]

This is certainly not a conventional temptation of the tower.
It is not even a temptation in the ordinary sense at all. Milton
says specifically that Satan has not come back with a "new
device: they *all* were spent," and makes it clear that he is trying "*another* method" to determine whether Christ is God or
man. The whole episode, in fact, has become simply a last
desperate test of identity, Milton's resolution of the doubt
motif. But the scene on the pinnacle is so brief and so highly
condensed that it is a little difficult to see at first glance in
just what this test was to consist. Newton and Calton argued
in the eighteenth century that Satan challenged Christ to prove
his divinity either by miraculously standing on the pinnacle
(a pointed spire), or by miraculously floating to the ground
unhurt. Since Christ was now in a position where he had to do
one or the other, he chose to stand.[59] Gilbert and Tillyard have
more recently suggested a different reading of the passage: the
devil never thought that Christ would be able to stand on
the pinnacle; he expected him to fall, and by falling to settle
the problem of his identity. If he were the Son of God, the

[58] *P. R.*, 4. 546-80.
[59] *Paradise Regained*, ed. Newton, pp. 193-95.

angels would save him; if he were not, he would die. "But something greater happens. Christ does not fall: he stands; and it is Satan, his period of power ended, who falls." [60] The modern theory is almost certainly the right one, since, as Gilbert sensibly points out, Christ ought not to accept one of the alternatives offered him by Satan. If the devil must needs get what he wants, it should obviously not be in any manner which he has anticipated, or which gratifies him in the least. Rather, just as he is gloating over the final successful cornering of his victim, the scheme should suddenly go wrong, the experiment blow up in his face, and his " triumphals," in Milton's own words, prove "joyless" because they bring him nothing but ruin and desperation and dismay.

Milton's reasons for adopting this peculiar conception of the *mitte te deorsum* must be a matter of conjecture. We do, however, know something of the problems he thought he faced, the materials he had to work with, and the final results which appear in *Paradise Regained*. Guided by these points of reference, we may, as children sometimes make pictures by drawing lines from dot to dot on a sheet of paper, possibly arrive at some rough and sketchy idea of what went on in his mind.

In the first place, he must certainly, at one time or another, have seriously considered writing the episode in accordance with the traditional view of the temptation of the tower. The work of the Renaissance theologians shows how well-established, how almost unquestioned, that view was in his day; the statement in *The Christian Doctrine* proves that it was acceptable to him. Then why should he have altered it? The answer which at once comes to mind is that he did so to provide a proper resolution of the doubt motif, because he was dissatisfied with the widespread assumption that Satan was left in ignorance at the conclusion of the temptation. But in that case he had, ready to his hand, the alternative theory that Satan realized the truth when Christ became angry and compelled his obedience after the offer of the kingdoms. [61] True, this hypothesis was less popular than the other, but Milton may well have known it. Even if he did not, he was quite capable of working out the

[60] Tillyard, p. 327. See also Gilbert, pp. 609-10.
[61] See Chapter III, pp. 34-35.

same solution for himself. Or he might have invented an entirely new incident of his own to deal with the point, as he had already done in the case of the banqueting scene. In either event, he could have avoided sacrificing the temptation of the tower.

There is also another and more probable answer to the question. He could hardly treat the temptation of the kingdoms exhaustively and categorically, as he planned, without dwelling on the ambitious man's desire for mere glory, mob-adulation, adoration even; and if so, it was difficult to see how the temptation of the tower could be presented without repeating a good deal of the same material. Anxious to avoid this offence, but unwilling to curtail his plans for the *regna omnia mundi*, he then hit upon the expedient of devising some new version of the pinnacle scene and leaving the matter of vain glory with its attendant sin of presumption to be taken up fully and wholly under the heading of the kingdoms. This is an attractive and plausible explanation, perhaps even the right one, and almost certainly part of the right one. But the conventional view of the temptation of the tower was so firmly entrenched that it was unlikely to be discarded in any such cavalier fashion for what was, after all, only one out of many forms of ambition; we would rather expect a seventeenth-century writer either to give up that particular section of the *regna omnia mundi*, or to resign himself to some inevitable repetition, perhaps preventing it insofar as was possible by focussing the *mitte te deorsum* on the sort of vain glory which is satisfied only with actual worship, and the *regna omnia mundi* on that which is content with common fame and ordinary applause. If he had already decided on a new and unorthodox pinnacle scene, then of course the possibility of working the old temptation of the tower into the *regna omnia mundi* might appear as a heaven-sent solution to the resulting theological difficulties; but at any event, he would hardly have abandoned the conventional view for no better reason than to build up the temptation of the kingdoms a little, unless he had been under additional pressure of some sort or other.

The way Milton handles the subject, however, suggests strongly that he *was* under such pressure. The whole final section of the poem, beginning with the storm scene, is curiously different from those which precede it: it is swift-moving, violent, dramatic, and condensed sometimes almost to the point of ambiguity. We cannot hope to share the full effect it would have on a seventeenth-century reader, even one prepared for something irregular by Milton's handling of the *regna omnia mundi*; but it still retains a measure of its power to startle and shock. Stopford Brooke went so far as to call it "theatrical" and conclude that "here Milton is driven into sensationalism because he does not understand his subject." [62] The chances are, however, that Milton knew exactly what he was doing. If his work suddenly became sensational, it must have reached a point where he felt that sensationalism was called for; and it is at least arguable that he was right. Brooke complained that he gave his third temptation only thirty lines, in comparison with the nine hundred he lavished on the second; [63] but Brooke cannot have seriously attempted to visualize the consequences of adding yet another nine hundred lines of subtle debate to a poem even now attacked chiefly on the ground that it is so overloaded with argument. Thoroughly as both Milton and his audience enjoyed theological dialectic, and freely as he intended to use it in *Paradise Regained*, he was still a creative writer keenly aware how soon one may have too much even of a good thing, and how many promising works have been ruined simply because their infatuated authors did not know where to stop. While he would never have been so vulgar as to reflect that he must not kill his cat by choking it with butter, he was doubtless deeply concerned over the flatness and monotony unavoidable if the poem were to consist of *nothing* but one elaborate and conscientious discussion relentlessly following another.

It was then, I believe, that he finally conceived the drastic idea of lightening this load of argument by amalgamating the old temptation of the tower with the *regna omnia mundi*, and making something spectacular out of the pinnacle scene to bring the poem up with a round turn. The work of the Renaissance theologians had already shown how breath-taking and dramatic the pinnacle scene might be made, if a writer were not pulled up at every point by the consideration due the sin of vainglorious presumption. But once that sin was otherwise

[62] Brooke, p. 158.   [63] *Ibid.*, p. 158.

provided for, and the *mitte te deorsum* reduced to a mere situation — Christ precariously erect on some dizzy height of the temple, with the devil at his shoulder and hideous depths below, what was Milton to do with the episode? The danger and fearfulness of the Lord's position might well suggest to him what they later suggested to Eliot — that the devil was trying to break Christ's nerve and make him afraid. Such a hypothesis would be all the more attractive because it fell in so well with the familiar theory that after Satan's efforts to delude Christ had failed, he returned to tempt him "violently" with the terror of pain and danger. A scene of that kind would necessarily be a very striking one; it would build up the dramatic ending needed after so much steady debate; it would enable Milton to cover every form of attack which Satan made on Christ; and it would provide some sort of theological underpinning for an episode which would otherwise lie completely outside the tradition. There were certain objections to be overcome: it was generally assumed that the devil at that time did nothing but persuade, and again, that the temptations by violence properly belonged to the period of the Passion. But once the three formal temptations by persuasion were over, any that followed would necessarily be of the other sort; moreover, he could treat the scene as a kind of curtain-raiser to the Passion, portending the future, and put words into Satan's mouth which would make the point quite clear.

But if the *mitte te deorsum* could easily be turned into a temptation by violence, it could be turned still more easily into an identity test and discovery scene of equally dramatic potentialities, but better substantiated by both the tradition and the text. The episode had long been regarded as an attempt on Satan's part to determine whether Christ was really the Son of God through his ability or inability to fall from the tower unhurt. Once the accompanying temptation was removed, it was only natural to consider the scene as wholly an identity test; and with the corollary removal of the essential condition that the Lord go down of his own free will, the idea of making the fall involuntary would readily occur to any author familiar with Renaissance interpretations of the word "pinnacle," especially the one which defined it as a sharp golden spire of the kind described by Josephus, where not even the birds could

secure a footing. The nature of the identity test would probably be enough in itself to suggest the nature of the discovery
scene — a complete reversal of Satan's every expectation; but
if at that moment Milton happened to recall some Renaissance
print or woodcut which showed Christ standing and the devil
plunging down in midair from the pinnacle, it would certainly
help to explain why he made both test and discovery what
he did.

The episode as he finally conceived it, however, did not
admit of being treated as *any* sort of temptation, even by
violence. The pinnacle is not merely a dangerous place which
Christ might stand on through courage or slip from through
cowardice: Satan's only intention in placing him there is to
make the fall inevitable. As a result, the formal temptation
by violence had to be pushed back and given independent
treatment in the storm scene, though it remains closely associated with the *mitte te deorsum* and is of much the same
character: a direct, crude, and furious attempt to get what is
wanted by force, at considerable peril to the victim. On the
other hand, it is possible (though less probable) that Milton
never thought of the pinnacle scene in connection with the
temptation by violence, but added the latter merely to build
up the dramatic ending still further or to fill in every form of
attack Satan made on the Lord.

That is the trouble with reconstructions of this sort: we
know what considerations were likely to occur to a man with
Milton's problem and his knowledge of theology, but not in
what sequence they entered his mind or what relation they had
to one another. All we can do is arrange the various integers
in what seems their logical order of occurrence or importance,
and hope for the best. But the only thing which is practically
certain is that the present unorthodox form of the *mitte te
deorsum* comes, in the last analysis, from its author's determination to introduce action and avoid overweighting the poem
with argument: there is no other wholly satisfactory explanation of either the conception or the style. The modern reader
may privately feel that the result is a pitiful instance of too
little too late; but in the seventeenth century it must have
represented a certain triumph of Milton the creative artist over
Milton the scholar and thinker.

The triumph, however, was a limited one: if the machinations of the creative artist were to hold their own, either in Milton's eyes or those of his audience, they would have to be somehow confirmed and justified by the scholar and thinker. There were very grave objections to any such treatment of the *mitte te deorsum*; and unless Milton was prepared to join the Trapps and Eliots on the lunatic fringe of contemporary theology, it was necessary to pay some attention to them. Anyone familiar with the tradition can see what they were. The new version of the pinnacle scene required the substitution of the Luke order for the more popular and universally approved one given by Matthew. Furthermore, it made Satan's suggestion and Christ's reply ridiculous and incomprehensible. Finally, it did away with the conventional temptation of the tower and as a result destroyed the triple equation.

We already know something of the way Milton dealt with the last and most serious difficulty—by working the essential temptation of vainglorious presumption into the *regna omnia mundi*. But we have still to consider how this expedient would affect his version of the triple equation. Obviously, there could no longer be any question of neatly parcelling out the world, the flesh, and the devil between the three temptations, one to each. However, at least one commentator who discarded the conventional *mitte te deorsum* had already hit upon the idea of making the *regna omnia mundi* a combined temptation of the world, the flesh, and the devil; and while it is too much to suppose that Milton knew or was influenced by Trapp's work, the line of thought Trapp had followed is the one which would inevitably open before any Renaissance writer confronted by the same problem. But Milton's mind was keener than his predecessor's, and the solution he reached more complete and ingenious. Like Trapp, he treats the *regna omnia mundi* as the temptation of both the world and the devil, but preserves the distinction between the two—and even the spirit of the Luke equation—by retaining the *mitte te deorsum* sin as the peculiar offence of Satan, and associating it only with that form of human ambition which most closely approximates the *eritis sicut dii* and the original crime of the devil. The kingdoms themselves — the countries he actually shows Christ from the mountain — are likewise treated very much as they are in the Luke equation: as the simple temptation of the *world*:

> The world thou hast not seen, much less her glory,
> Empires, and Monarchs, and thir radiant Courts . . .
> But I will bring thee where thou soon shalt quit
> Those rudiments, and see before thine eyes
> The Monarchies of the Earth, thir pomp and state.[64]

It should also be noted that Milton does not attach the unlawful delights of the flesh simply and unequivocally to the *regna omnia mundi*, as Trapp does. Worldly temptations which are also physical luxuries form part of the attractions of Rome; but the mere indulgence of physical appetite is carefully distinguished from these and separately treated in the banqueting scene. The banqueting scene, however, immediately precedes the *regna omnia mundi*, though not actually part of it. In a sense, therefore, Milton may be said to present a combined temptation of the world, the flesh, and the devil, since the three sins which typify them—gluttony, vain glory, and avarice—all appear together on the same day.

It may be argued that this arrangement would have satisfied nobody but a Papist who did not particularly care whether all the chief incidents of the poem were drawn into the basic pattern of the triple equation. But Milton seems to have anticipated the difficulty. In the poem, as we now have it, each day is devoted to a different *type* of temptation: temptation by necessity—the Protestant *dic ut lapides*; temptation by pleasure —the world, the flesh, and the devil in their attractive and alluring shapes; and temptation by violence—Milton's own addition of a trial not usually included with the others. The first was the Protestant version of the temptation of the flesh. The second might be loosely described as a temptation of the world, since all earthly pleasures are by definition "things of this world" in the widest sense of the word, though within the definition it is possible to discriminate between those of the flesh, those of the devil, and those of the "world" in its technical sense. The key text from John, in fact, makes exactly this distinction: "For all that is in the world, the lust of the flesh, the lust of the eyes, and the pride of life, is not of the Father,

[64] *P. R.*, 3. 236-46.

but is of the world." [65] The third could with some justice be
called a temptation of the devil, since it is a direct attack
by Satan, and, together with the *mitte te deorsum*, represents the exercise of his naked power in its most terrifying
and ugly form. [66] Milton's equation appears, therefore, to be a
combination of two: the first broad and general, comprehending all the incidents of the poem, carrying the reader through
the various stages in their proper order from the flesh to the
devil; and within this one, another, more limited and traditional, dealing specifically with *concupiscentia carnis, concupiscentia oculorum*, and *superbia vitae*. This pattern is not in
every respect satisfactory: the parallels between the temptations of Christ and Adam could not reasonably extend beyond
those of the second day, nor does Milton attempt to draw any,
though the events of the third day are definitely linked with
and foreshadow the final struggle by which Christ wholly
undid the work of Satan and set Adam free. But as a pattern,
Milton's final arrangement had other virtues besides that of
necessity. It preserved the best features of both Catholic and
Protestant equations, while avoiding the unacceptable theological implications of the one and the ambiguous half-measures
of the other. At the same time, it covered more forms of temptation than either, and discriminated between them more deli-
cately and exactly. One feels that it would have at least silenced
(if not convinced) any except the most bigoted and hidebound
seventeenth-century reader.

That reader might still have objected, however, to the position of Milton's *mitte te deorsum* and accused him of violating
the plain meaning of the dialogue given in the text. But the
difficulty about the order of the temptations was a very minor
one. Luke's arrangement might not be so satisfactory as Matthew's, but it was there in the Bible and hence quite authori-
tative enough to be used by any writer who needed it. Satan's
suggestion and Christ's reply constituted more serious problems. If the Lord has been brought to the pinnacle only to
fall from it, why should the devil tell him to cast himself down,

---

[65] I John 2:16.

[66] It is interesting to note that God the Father speaks of Christ's overcoming
" Satanic *strength* / And all the world, and mass of sinful flesh," (1.161-62) not
" Satanic *pride*," as one might have expected.

as if he had any choice in the matter? Milton meets this question by stating that Satan speaks "in scorn" and by making it clear that he does not actually mean what he says—for since the pinnacle is one of Josephus's gilded spires, the words, "There stand, if thou wilt stand; to stand upright / Will ask thee skill," must be mere sarcasm, intended to show the real nature of what follows: "If not to stand, cast thyself down." It is more difficult to understand what he made of Christ's reply, which is given practically verbatim, without qualification or addition. If the Lord was not to fall of his own free will, he would be justly entitled to the protection of the angels, and in no way deliberately "making trial" of God; therefore, if his answer is interpreted in the usual terms, it is meaningless.

It makes sense, in fact, only if we suppose that Milton thought of it as Hilary, Pseudo-Chrysostom, and Walafridus Strabus did: *Me Dominum tuum non tentabis*, and intended his readers to assume that "Tempt not the Lord thy God, he said, and stood," really meant, "Make not trial of *me*, the Lord your God." That remarkable critic Calton was already arguing almost two hundred years ago that the line would admit of no other interpretation,[67] even though he apparently reached this conclusion by pure logic, unsupported by the evidence that in the seventeenth century his reading was an acknowledged version of the Gospel text itself—a fact which would explain not only how Milton came to think of it, but why he could expect his audience to understand it. It had, too, the further advantage of fitting perfectly into his rendering of the situation. Satan, of course, recognizes the Lord's real nature because he does not fall. But it is entirely appropriate (and highly dramatic) that this miracle should be accompanied by an unequivocal announcement of Christ's identity, at the moment when he finally exerts his divine powers to stand and his authority from Heaven to rid himself of the devil. Moreover, the chief objections which Taylor brings against any such reading of the verse do not really apply here: Christ is no longer acting under the peculiar conditions of the temptation, which made it necessary for him to speak and behave wholly as man; because the episode therefore has no exemplary func-

[67] Calton, note to 4. 561 of *Paradise Regained*, ed. Newton, pp. 194-95.

tion, his words can certainly be " restricted to this particular occasion "; and Satan does not go on attacking him, as Milton, unlike Taylor, is following the order in Luke. True, he had already subscribed to the more orthodox view of the text in *The Christian Doctrine*, but we have no reason to suppose that he would object to contradicting himself if the circumstances required it, since he apparently thought nothing of presenting one explanation of the sons of God's affair with the daughters of men in *Paradise Lost*, and quite another in *Paradise Regained*.

Still, in view of the fact that the tradition proves this particular version of the *non tentabis* was by no means so well known or firmly established as the alternative, it is rather curious that Milton did not try to prevent any possibility of confusion by writing plainly, " Make not trial of me," or at least adding something to show his readers that Christ's reply was to be understood in that particular sense, if he actually meant it to be. But the really strong argument against any such interpretation of the line is the sheer difficulty of believing that Milton could ever have brought himself to accept it. When we think of the pages and pages in *The Christian Doctrine* devoted to explaining away those embarrassing texts of Scripture which actually do identify Christ with the Father, it seems almost incredible that the writer, under any circumstances whatever, would consider permitting Christ to call himself God on the strength of a verse which even the most conventional theologians usually held to refer to the Father alone.

Strangely enough, however, it may have been the very intensity of Milton's heretical opinions that made him feel it was permissible to adopt the variant reading of " Tempt not the Lord thy God." As he points out in *The Christian Doctrine*, the hypothesis that the Son is essentially one with the Father rests on the fact that he is given the title of God in the Bible:

It must be understood . . . that God imparted to the Son as much as he pleased of the divine nature, nay of the divine substance itself, care being taken not to confound the substance with the whole essence. . . . Since, however, Christ not only bears the name of the only begotten Son of God, but is also several times called in Scripture God, notwithstanding the universal doctrine that there is but one God, it appeared to many . . . that there was an inconsistency in this; which gave rise to an hypothesis no less strange than repugnant to reason, namely, that the Son, although personally and numerically another, was yet essentially one with the Father, and thus the unity of God was preserved.[68]

Milton therefore attempts to refute this theory by arguing that the mere title of God does not imply identity with the Godhead, and by citing a long list of texts to prove it had been given to angels, to judges, to the whole house of David, to all the saints, to a false god, to Dagon, to single idols, and to Moses, as well as to God the Father. It was, however, more especially reserved for those who acted as His deputies on earth: judges, for instance, "because they occupy the place of God to a certain degree in the administration of judgment," and angels, "because as heavenly messengers they bear the appearance of the divine glory and person, and even speak in the very words of the Deity." And if, he concludes, "the name of God is not unfrequently ascribed, by the will and concession of God the father, even to angels and men, how much more then to the only begotten Son, the image of the Father," [69] who is indeed divine, the one manifestation of God Himself, the agent through whom He made and governs creation, even though "to be God, and to be in the bosom of God the Father—to be God, and to be from God—to be the one invisible God, and to be the only-begotten and visible, are things so different that they cannot be predicated of one and the same essence." [70]

In other words, "the name and presence of God is used to imply his vicarious power and might resident in the Son." [71] This hypothesis is Milton's trump card, the favorite arrow in his quiver, the clinching argument on which he usually falls back when he has exhausted every other means of persuading the reader to accept his version of a disputed text. He uses it to help make his case against the orthodox interpretation of Romans 9:5, "Christ who is over all, God blessed forever. Amen":

Supposing that the words are spoken of the Son, they have nothing to do with his essence, but only intimate that divine honor is com-

---

[68] Milton, *Works*, 14. 193-95.
[69] *Ibid.*, pp. 243-52, *passim.*
[70] *Ibid.*, pp. 337-39.
[71] *Ibid.*, p. 301.

municated to the Son by the Father, and particularly that he is called God; which is nothing more than what has been already fully shown by other arguments.[72]

The same note is sounded again in the discussion of I John 5:20, "This is the true God and eternal life":

We are not obliged to say of Christ what the Scriptures do not say. The Scriptures call him "God," but not "him that is the true God"; why are we not at liberty to acquiesce in the same distinction? At all events, *he* is not to be called a false God, to whom, as to his beloved Son, he that is the true God has communicated his divine power and glory.[73]

Since, therefore, Milton seems quite willing to grant Christ the *title* of God (for what that title may be worth after he finishes defining it), we have no real grounds for supposing that he would absolutely refuse to let Jesus tell the devil that he is the Lord his God, particularly at a moment when he is actually exercising "the vicarious power and might resident in the Son." When the Son puts on his Father's authority in *Paradise Lost*, Milton speaks of him simply as "God"; and it is not beyond possibility that he may have seen fit to stretch a point and grant him the same privilege in *Paradise Regained*. Of course, it is one thing to lay down a principle with an eye to explaining a text which makes Christ God; it is quite another to apply the same principle to a text when its effect will be to make God Christ. Milton would probably never have thought of so interpreting "Thou shalt not tempt the Lord thy God," under ordinary circumstances; but since the circumstances were not ordinary, and there was literally no other way out of his difficulties, he was likely to do what he usually did when driven to the wall in *The Christian Doctrine*: admit that Jesus had a right to the title, and console himself with the familiar reflection: "Supposing that the words are spoken of the Son, they have nothing to do with his essence, but only intimate that divine honor is communicated to the Son by the Father . . ."

No doubt he adopted the expedient with some reluctance; but we are hardly entitled to assume that he rejected it alto-

---

[72] *Ibid.*, pp. 261-63.
[73] *Ibid.*, pp. 271-73. For other examples of the same argument, see p. 217; pp. 267-69; pp. 293-95.

gether and merely let the *non tentabis* stand, because he could neither make anything of it nor remove it from his work, even though no longer compatible with his treatment of the subject. For merely to let it stand would in itself be the equivalent of endorsing the variant reading, since some, if not all, of his readers would certainly remember it and assume that the line meant, "Make not trial of me," — indeed, what else could they think? It may perhaps be argued that he at least refrained from making its meaning explicit, though he could not prevent instructed readers from understanding it in that sense, and could not have defended it on any other grounds if his version of the pinnacle scene were attacked. But surely that would have been a rather shuffling and nonsensical compromise with his conscience. The chances are that he simply assumed that his audience would either be familiar with the tradition or capable of working out the meaning of the line from the material supplied them. He did not, after all, anticipate readers who would be ignorant of the one or uninterested in the other.

CHAPTER VIII

MINOR TRADITIONS

The seventeenth-century reader was likely to be familiar not
only with the major hypotheses about the temptation, but with
a number of minor traditions as well. These are frequently
interesting or amusing, though too unimportant to deserve
consideration at length. They are therefore presented here as
a group.

The Wild Beasts

Mark is the only Evangelist who asserts that there were
animals in the wilderness; he writes that Christ was "there . . .
with the wild beasts."[1] Some exegetes held that he included
the verse merely to show that the place was solitary and unin-
habited: "ut non desertum domesticum, sed vere desertum
intelligeremus."[2] Others went on to draw from this fact such
useful lessons as that it is better to be among wild beasts than
wicked men,[3] or that Satan most often tempts the devout when
they are alone.[4] Still others pointed out that while the beasts
were dangerous and ferocious—Lapide describes them as lions,
wolves, pards, and serpents[5] — they did not attempt to harm
Christ, because they recognized in him the same perfection
which had made them respect man before the fall: "he was safe
among them as *Adam* in innocency."[6] A few even went so far
as to suggest that they actually came and paid homage to the
Lord; Giles Fletcher, for instance, paints a most fantastic and
charming picture of the animals frolicking about their Master
very much as they once had in the Garden of Eden:

---

[1] Mark 1:3.

[2] Cajetanus, col. 25. See also Calvin, *Commentarii*, pp. 53-54; Marlorate, pp. 56-
57; I. H., p. 266; Woodhead, p. 108.

[3] Bale, sig. D2ʳ; Bede, *In Marci Evangelium Expositio*, col. 140; Wild, pp. 53-54.

[4] Chrysostom, col. 209; Euthymius Zigabenus, col. 174; Theophylactus, *Enarratio
in Evangelium Marci, Patr. Gr.* 123, col. 499; Perkins, pp. 24-25. Chrysostom and
Perkins both note that the devil tempted Eve when she was by herself, a point also
emphasized by Milton in *Paradise Lost*.

[5] Lapide, p. 98.

[6] Cradock, p. 39. See also T. Taylor, pp. 43-44; Euthymius Zigabenus, col. 775.

Downe felle the Lordly Lions angrie mood,
And he himselfe felle downe, in congies lowe;
Bidding him welcome to his wastefull wood,
Sometime he kist the grasse whear he did goe,
And, as to wash his feete he well did knowe,
　　With fauning tongue he lickt away the dust,
　　And every one would neerest to him thrust,
And every one, with new, forgot his former lust.

Unmindful of himselfe, to minde his Lord,
The Lamb stood gazing by the Tyger's side,
As though betweene them they had made accord,
And on the Lions back the goate did ride,
Forgetfull of the roughnes of his hide,
　　If he stood still, their eyes upon him bayted,
　　If walk't, they all in order on him wayted,
And when he slep't, they as his watch themselves conceited.[7]

But to carry the matter as far as Fletcher does was apparently considered an error in judgment, for Thomas Taylor writes:

That the wilde beasts should come and doe homage to him their Lord, as they did to *Adam* . . . is a devise of man's braine, for although Christ deserued honour . . . from all creatures . . . yet this is not the time and place to receive it: yea they forget, that Christ went *into the wilderness* to be humbled in a special manner.[8]

And Perkins criticizes the hypothesis in much the same terms: Christ, as he puts it, "came not to this end into the world, but rather to take on him the shape of a seruant."[9] Most commentators who touched on the theme were therefore content to observe that Christ, like Adam, went unmolested by the beasts because like Adam, he was perfect man; and some simply ascribed his safety to his character, without mentioning Adam at all:

Christs innocence commanded the wilde beasts into obedience; muzled the Bears mouth, brake the Tygers teeth, blunted the Boars tuske, pared the Lions paws.[10]

---

[7] Fletcher, 1. 40-41. Cf. Dyke, p. 235: "not offering violence to Christ, but acknowledging the Image of God in him, as once to *Adam* in his innocency"; Lapide, p. 577.

[8] T. Taylor, p. 43.

[9] Perkins, p. 24.

[10] Fuller, p. 28. See also Aretius, *Commentarii in Evangelium Secundum Marcum*, pp. 43-44; and Allen, p. 79: "the wilde and sauage beasts durst not approach to hurt him."

Milton belongs to this last group. He says of the beasts only that

> they at [Christ's] sight grew mild,
> Nor sleeping him nor waking harmed; his walk
> The fiery serpent fled and noxious worm;
> The lion and fierce tiger glared aloof.[11]

This treatment of the subject is certainly less colorful and touching than Giles Fletcher's naive picture of the riotously happy crowd of animals forgetting their natural antipathies and rejoicing in unity at the feet of Christ. But, as Taylor and Perkins had already implied, that picture belonged properly to the very end of the story, when the lion and the lamb lay down together in the New Jerusalem, and not to its grim beginning in the wilderness, with all the work of redemption still to do. Furthermore, Milton evidently wished to retain that emphasis on the dreadful solitude of Christ which was already a part of the tradition, and therefore deliberately avoided any suggestion of companionship or comfort which might serve to mitigate his condition. The wild beasts in *Paradise Regained* grow " mild," but they do not come near the Lord; they either " flee " or " glare aloof." It is entirely natural and fitting that they should show so much respect for Christ, but equally fitting that under the circumstances they should show no more.

The Wilderness

The Evangelists do not name the wilderness where the temptation occurred; and many commentators do not speculate about its location, perhaps because they felt, as Perkins has it, that " seeing the holy Ghost does not shew what wilderness it was, we are not curiously to inquire after it, but onely know it was a desert and solitary place." [12] Others, however, including Perkins himself, prefer to be more specific and attempt to determine exactly which region was meant. One school held that it was a small wilderness between Jerusalem and Jericho, which Lapide calls Quarantana, and Chemnitius, Quarentena.[13] Chemnitius adds that the place was mountainous, an observa-

---

[11] *P. R.*, 1. 310-13.   [12] Perkins, p. 13.
[13] Lapide, p. 98; Chemnitius, p. 37. Chemnitius, though he gives the theory, does not himself accept it. Perkins (p. 13) lists it as a possible alternative to his own.

tion which explains why I. H. calls it "a very high hill, called
Quarenta, distant from the place of his baptism some four
myle."[14] Luca says that both mountain and desert were named
Quarentana, and were not far from the other mountain where
the temptation of the kingdoms took place.[15] St. Paschasius
Radbertus and Mayer agree that the wilderness lay between
Jerusalem and Jericho, but call it Damin, because that was
where the man fell among thieves according to the parable,
which they took to be a presentation of the temptation on the
allegorical level, with Christ (the good Samaritan) rescuing
Adam (the man) from Satan (the thieves).[16] Another group
of commentators, however, maintained that the site of the
temptation was really the "great wilderness, commonly called
The Desert of Arabia,"[17] where Elijah fasted and the Jews
wandered for the forty years. As Chemnitius and Leigh point
out, the place in Biblical times had no local name like the
wilderness of Judea, and therefore would be given none by the
Evangelists. Furthermore, as Trapp suggests, "*Moses & Elias*
had fasted [there] before," a fact which would make the spot
especially appropriate to the temptation, because, as we know,
it was the fasts of Moses and Elijah which were supposed to
have set the precedent for the *quadraginta dies.*[18]

It was evidently this last consideration which led Milton to
accept the theory that the wilderness was the desert of Arabia.
He makes no parade of identifying it as such; the fact emerges
casually during the discussion at the first temptation. But he
seizes upon, and builds into his work, the one detail which gives
the site of the temptation real meaning and importance; and
he brings out, much more clearly than any commentator, what
effect it had on the mind of Christ. As the Lord tells Satan:

> Man lives not by bread only, but each word
> Proceeding from the mouth of God, who fed
> Our fathers *here* with manna; in the Mount
> Moses was forty days, nor eat nor drank,

---

[14] I. H., p. 266.
[15] Luca, col. 537.
[16] St. Paschasius Radbertus, col. 186; Mayer, p. 77.
[17] Manton, p. 9. See also Trapp, p. 30; Leigh, p. 8; Chemnitius, p. 37; and Perkins,
p. 13.
[18] See Chapter II, p. 16.

> And forty days Elijah without food
> *Wandred this barren waste; the same I now.*
> Why dost thou then suggest to me distrust? [19]

" *The devil showed unto him* — "

How did the devil contrive to *show* Christ all the kingdoms of the world from a single high mountain top? There was no one generally accepted answer to the question; but the various hypotheses suggested and discussed during the Middle Ages and the Renaissance may be summed up as follows:

1) It was, quite literally, all done with mirrors: Satan set up a series of glasses which reflected scenes from the first to the next in order, and so on until they reached the mountain.[20]

2) Satan made " a Scheme and representation unto him of the great and spacious Kingdomes of the Earth; and of all the Glory and beauty, as it were, set forth and spread before him in a large Map." [21]

3) The devil flew with Christ over the world, showing him the sights as they went.[22]

4) Satan so wrought upon Christ's imagination that he thought he was seeing the kingdoms.[23]

5) Christ made use of his own miraculous powers to see the kingdoms for himself.[24]

6) The devil pointed in the direction of the various quarters of the globe where the different kingdoms lay, told Christ their names, and described their splendors.[25]

---

[19] *P. R.*, 1. 349-55. Italics mine.

[20] Lapide, p. 106. Lapide lists the theory, but thinks it silly: " verum sic daemon aerem totum implesset speculis, quae se inuicem impedievissent, nec suffecissent ad videndum omnia."

[21] Woodhead, p. 118. See also Coccejus, 4. 9. Cf. Plate V.

[22] Lapide, p. 106; Blackwood, pp. 102-103. Both reject the theory on the ground that the text says specifically the temptation took place on the mountain.

[23] Lapide, p. 106; Blackwood, p. 103; Jansen, col. 536. All three reject the theory on the ground that the temptation was *foris non intus*; the devil had no power over Christ's imagination.

[24] Bilson, pp. 308-9. This hypothesis may be Bilson's own invention; it is not listed even by Lapide and Blackwood, who go into the question most thoroughly. In any event, it cannot have been popular, since any overt display of Christ's miraculous powers was tantamount to a revelation of his real identity and inappropriate in itself because he was undertaking the temptation as a man.

[25] Euthymius Zigabenus, col. 178; St. Thomas Aquinas, *Summa Theologica*, pars

7) The kingdoms were mirages or visions which the devil raised "in aere a se varie condensato, per varias fulgoris solis refractiones," so that Christ saw them as we see a rainbow, quite distinctly, but without any illusion about their reality.[26]

8) The kingdoms were not real, but allegorical.[27]

Of the seven hypotheses based on the assumption that the kingdoms were real, the first was obviously fantastic; the second seems to have attracted little attention; and the third, fourth, and fifth conflicted either with the text or with other parts of the tradition. The sixth was evidently popular, but open to the objection made by Lapide: that it did not account for the fact that the devil showed Christ the glories as well as the kingdoms. During the Renaissance, however, this difficulty was frequently overcome by combining the sixth with some form of the seventh, as Blackwood did:

I lean to the [belief] that the Devil from that high mountain showed Christ onely the coast and situation of all the quarters and kingdoms of the World, saying, this is *Europe*, this is *Africk*, this *Asia*, this *England*, this *France*, *Spain*, &c. And because he shewed him the glory of them, it's like the Devil like a Painter represented unto Christ all the glorious things that were in every Kingdom, by thickening of the air, wherein the Devil made certain Images of things which were no less apparent to Christ, than Colours in the Rain-bowe to us, for neither were the eys, nor imagination of Christ deluded.[28]

Jansen and Luca agree with Blackwood, but prefer to argue that instead of revealing the glories of the kingdoms by raising mirages, Satan may have employed some form of the scientific principles of magnification which were the subject of so much experiment and controversy during the Renaissance: "potuit autem hoc efficere . . . prospectivae sive opticae artis vi, quam

3, quaest. 41, art. 4. Bilson (p. 308) gives the theory as a possible alternative to his own; Lapide (p. 106) lists but rejects it because the text says that Satan *showed* the glories as well as the kingdoms.

[26] Lapide, p. 106; he thinks this solution the correct one. See also Bilson, pp. 309-10; Poole, p. 640; and Perkins, pp. 88-89. Pseudo-Chrysostom (cols. 686-87) also describes the kingdoms as seen "per fictas aerias formas," and in *Twelfth Century Homilies* (p. 103), the writer also says Satan used specious arts to show them by means of illusions.

[27] See Chapter V, p. 61.

[28] Blackwood, p. 103. See also Fuller, pp. 133-35; Cradock, p. 41; Manton, pp. 124-26.

non ignorat (qua arte ab hominibus conficiuntur inspicilla, quae longissime distantes res oculis exactissime subjiciunt) ." [29]

Milton's treatment of the question most nearly resembles Jansen and Luca's. He follows the sixth hypothesis as far as he can: the devil tells Christ in what relation to the mountain the different kingdoms lie; he describes three of them at length; and he apparently brings the Lord to a vantage-point from which he can actually see the first one for himself. But he cannot show him Rome and Athens as he had Parthia, without moving on to other mountains; he is therefore obliged to exhibit them

> presented to [Christ's] eyes
> Above the height of mountains interposed.
> By what strange parallax or optic skill
> Of vision multiplied through air, or glass
> Of telescope, were curious to inquire.[30]

Since Milton had once claimed acquaintance with Galileo and had twice alluded to his discoveries in *Paradise Lost*,[31] it is not surprising to find that he was evidently attracted by the pseudo-scientific explanation of Satan's methods. He alludes to it again in the description of Rome that follows, when Satan boasts that "well have I disposed / My airy microscope." [32] But he may also have had some feeling that the kingdoms were really mirages: the suggestion that they were shown by "optic skill of vision multiplied through air" reads like a reminiscence of the seventh hypothesis. It is clear, however, that he did not consider the matter a fit subject for the minute inquiry and ample theorizing some theologians had indulged in; and he deliberately kept his whole discussion of the topic as vague and indeterminate as he could.

---

[29] Luca, col. 538. See also Jansen, cols. 536-37. Luca adds that Satan may have used mirages as well as magnification. Leigh, too, may have been thinking of the magnification theory when he wrote (p. 104) that the kingdoms were shown by means of "optikes." Lapide notes (p. 106) that Toletus " putat daemonem species rerum remotissinarum, puta regnorum, vi sua perduxisse ad Christum Christique oculos, sicut ventus perflans vocem longius perducit, quam illa sine vento audiri posset "; but I have been unable to obtain the original, and the hypothesis as Lapide quotes it is too vague and obscure to amount to much.

[30] *P. R.*, 4. 38-42.
[31] *P. L.*, 1. 286-91; 5. 262.
[32] *P. R.*, 4. 56-57.

The Combat Images

Whenever the theologians of the Middle Ages or the Renaissance turn to imagery to describe the temptation, they almost invariably begin to think and write of it as if it were a struggle between rival warriors or athletes. Sometimes the analogy is merely suggested by the use of appropriate terminology, as it is when Bede refers to the desert as the "locum certaminis,"[33] or when Jerome calls Christ the "victor" and insists that he went into the wilderness "non invitus aut captus, sed voluntate pugnandi."[34] Sometimes the metaphor is explicit and elaborate. Luca, for instance, pictures Jesus as an invader determined to overthrow the kingdom of Satan, and the temptation as a battle by which he successfully establishes a sort of beach-head on the enemy territory.[35] Walafridus Strabus compares the temptation to the combat between David and Goliath, and Dyke to that between Michael and the Dragon.[36] Rupertus Abbas likens the Lord's conduct to that of a true prince, who fights in the vanguard of the battle to guide and inspire his followers by his own heroic example;[37] Lancelot Andrewes and many others warn their readers to regard themselves as young and inexperienced soldiers who have been permitted to watch a combat between their leader and their enemy, in order, as Andrewes puts it, "that we may be warned beforehand by seeing the strength of our adversary, and that also seeing the manner of his fight and of our Saviour's defence we may be instructed how to arm ourselves, and how to ward accordingly."[38] For, said Downame frankly, "we are but fresh water souldiers & white-livered; and therefore we had need to en-

[33] Bede, *In Matthaei Evangelium Expositio*, col. 18.
[34] St. Jerome, col. 31.
[35] Luca, col. 527.
[36] Walafridus Strabus, *Expositio in Quatuor Evangelia*, col. 870. The subtitle of Dyke's treatise on the temptation is "*Michael and the Dragon, or Christ tempted and Satan foyled*." It is interesting to note that in the Boxall-Coleridge-Richee manuscript of the *Speculum Humanae Salvationis* (ed. James, p. 22), one of the three scenes from the Old Testament used to balance the picture of the temptation is the struggle between Goliath and David. The other two are Daniel destroying Bel and the dragon, and David killing the lion and bear.
[37] Rupertus Abbas, col. 1547.
[38] Andrewes, p. 480. See also St. Augustine, *Sermo CXXIII*, col. 685; Euthymius Zigabenus, col. 174; Piscator, p. 57.

courage our selves . . . by looking on the victory of our chiefe Captaine."[39]

Again, Fuller begs his audience: "Seriously consider the eminencie of the persons; Generals seldom fight Duels as here, the Prince of Peace against the Prince of Darkness. . . . The success of some fights hath been in such a twilight, that after the battel ended with the swords of the soldiers, they have been begun with the pens of the Historians, disputing who got the better; . . . But here the Devil was quite routed, forsook the field, & after left our Saviour sole Conqueror."[40] Chrysostom compares Satan at the conclusion of the second temptation to a fighter mortally wounded and reeling on his feet,[41] while Pseudo-Chrysostom speaks of the third temptation as a final struggle in which the Lord, like a wrestler, sweeps up his opponent and pitches him violently down.[42] Even John Knox goes so far as to put into Christ's mouth a formal challenge to his adversary, in language that might have come direct from the *Morte d'Arthur*:

Sathan, thou gloriest of thy power and victorie over mankynd, that thair is nane abill to withstand thy assaltis nor eschape thy dart, but at a tyme or uthir thou givest him a wound! Lo, I am a man lyke to my brethren . . . tempt, try, and assalt me: I offer thee heir a place most convenient (the wildernes); thair salbe na mortall creature to comfort me against thy assaltis; thou sall have tyme sufficient, do what thow canst, I sal not flie the place of battell.[43]

And Daniel Dyke, having described the Lord in his title as Michael binding the Dragon, turns to a much more homely metaphor to celebrate his conquest:

The greater ods Satan had, the greater was the shame of his foyle; the greater the glory of Christ's victory, while he beats him in the desart, the place where he raignes & triumphs, *Luke* 8. 29, as it were a Cocke upon his owne dung-hill, and that in the weaknes, which hunger brought upon him.[44]

There was every reason why Milton should have taken kindly to this traditional conception of the temptation as a

---

[39] Downame, p. 15.   [42] Pseudo-Chrysostom, col. 688.
[40] Fuller, pp. 1-3.   [43] Knox, 4. 103.
[41] Chrysostom, col. 210.   [44] Dyke, p. 207.

duel. In the first place, the identification of debate with single combat was a figure of speech he liked, and had used occasionally in his younger days to dignify his own excursions into civil and religious controversy.[45] Moreover, it was obvious that an allegorical war with Satan on earth would provide an effective parallel to the literal war with Satan in heaven, and serve to maintain and point up the correspondence or balance of event between the earlier poem and the later that is so marked a feature of *Paradise Regained*. In Book Twelve of *Paradise Lost*, he had already toyed with the notion that the Redemption was comparable to a second defeat of Satan; but here Michael seems more concerned with warning Adam not to regard the combat as an actual conflict than with pointing out how like one it was to be:

> Dream not of thir fight,
> As of a Duel, or the local wounds
> Of head or heel: not therefore joynes the Son
> Manhood to God-head, with more strength to foil
> Thy enemie . . .
> Not by destroying Satan, but his works
> In thee and in thy Seed.[46]

In his later work, however, Milton picks up the duel-image and uses it again and again, especially at the beginning and end of the narrative, where he is particularly concerned with establishing the significance of the whole. It enters the poem with his first invocation to his muse:

> Thou Spirit who ledst this glorious Eremite
> Into the Desert, his Victorious Field

---

[45] See *Reason of Church Government*, where he compares a man fighting prelatry for the sake of the true church to a knight fighting a dragon for the sake of the King's daughter (*Works*, 3. 273); *The Doctrine and Discipline of Divorce*, where he challenges the opposition in very medieval terms:

> But if any one be truly and not pretendedly zealous for God's honor, here I call him forth, before men and angels, to use his best and most advised skill—

(*Works*, 4. 442); and *Areopagitica*, where the same metaphor is used to describe the best sort of free controversy:

> [He] calls out his adversary into the plain, offers him the advantage of wind and sun, if he pleases, only that he may try the matter by dint of argument.

(*Works*, 4. 347).

[46] *P. L.*, 12. 386-95.

Against the Spiritual Foe, and broughtst him thence
By proof the undoubted Son of God, inspire,
As thou art wont, my prompted Song else mute.[47]

The theme recurs in the Father's address to the angels:

I mean
To exercise him in the Wilderness,
There he shall first lay down the rudiments
Of his great warfare, e're I send him forth
To conquer Sin and Death, the two grand foes,
By Humiliation and strong Sufferance,[48]

and appears again in the hymn which immediately follows:

Victory and Triumph to the Son of God
Now entring his great duel, not of arms,
But to vanquish by wisdom hellish wiles.[49]

The rest of the combat-images are variations on the same
theme. In Book Four, Christ and Satan are compared to
wrestlers, in the manner of Pseudo-Chrysostom:

As when Earths Son *Antaeus* (to compare
Small things with greatest) in *Irassa* strove
With *Jove's Alcides*, and oft foil'd still rose,
Receiving from his mother Earth new strength,
Fresh from his fall, and fiercer grapple joyn'd,
Throttl'd at length in the Air, expir'd and fell;
So after many a foil the Tempter proud,
Renewing fresh assaults, amidst his pride
Fell whence he stood to see his Victor fall.[50]

It is also possible that Milton, like Knox, associated the temptation with feats of knight-errantry. The very beautiful and
famous metaphor applied to the ladies who appear with the
banquet—

---

[47] *P. R.*, 1. 8-12.
[48] *P. R.*, 1. 156-60.
[49] *P. R.*, 1. 173-76.
[50] *P. R.*, 4. 562-70. Milton may also have had wrestling in mind when he wrote
at the opening of Book Four that Satan stood " perplex'd," realizing that Christ is

far his over-match, who self-deceived
And rash, before-hand had no better weigh'd
The strength he was to cope with, or his own;

(4. 7-9); but the metaphor is not explicit enough to be assigned to any particular
category.

> Fairer then feign'd of old, or fabl'd since
> Of Fairy Damsels met in Forest wide
> By Knights of *Logres*, or of *Lyones*,
> *Lancelot or Pelleas, or Pellenore —* [51]

is not an obvious variant of the duel-image; but the implication
that Christ is the equivalent of Lancelot, or Pelleas, or Pelle-
nore—the questing warrior in a wilderness—is entirely conso-
nant with the tradition, and may well represent a subtle ex-
tension of it.

Finally, there is a strong suggestion throughout that Christ
is to be regarded as a lawful prince warring to regain his
patrimony from an unlawfully established tyrant. Satan is
repeatedly described as the lord of mankind *de facto*, and
Christ as the lord *de jure*.[52] At the second council of devils,
Satan, like Luca, calls him an invader of occupied territory:

> Such an Enemy
> Is ris'n to invade us, who no less
> Threat'ns then our expulsion down to Hell.[53]

And in the final anthem at the close of the poem, the angels
acclaim him as the "heir of both worlds," who has defeated
Satan's attempt to usurp his authority on earth precisely as
he had once defeated a similar attempt to usurp his authority
in heaven:

> still expressing
> The Son of God, with Godlike force indu'd
> Against th'Attempter of thy Fathers Throne,
> And Thief of Paradise; him long of old
> Thou didst debel, and down from Heav'n cast
> With all his Army, now thou hast aveng'd
> Supplanted *Adam*, and by vanquishing
> Temptation, hast regain'd lost Paradise,
> And frustrated the conquest fraudulent. . . .
> Hail Son of the most High, heir of both worlds,
> Queller of Satan, on thy glorious work
> Now enter, and begin to save mankind.[54]

It is this passage that most clearly marks off Milton's use of

[51] *P. R.*, 2. 358-61.
[52] See for example, 1. 47-50; 1. 115-18; 1. 124-25; 1. 254; 3. 441; 4. 183.
[53] *P. R.*, 2. 126-28.
[54] *P. R.*, 4. 601-35.

the combat-images from that of his predecessors. In the work of Luca, Knox, Pseudo-Chrysostom, and the others, they remain mere decorations, casual illustrations, introduced simply to give color and vividness to the facts of the immediate situation. Those in *Paradise Regained*, though richer and more numerous, seem at first to be little more. And then, with the recognition that the inward and spiritual conflict in the wilderness has been the counterpart and the continuation of the outward and visible conflict that began in heaven, all the scattered and various images strewn through the poem suddenly fall into line — take on coherence, significance, power — and become an integral and organic part of the single stupendous conception that binds *Paradise Lost* and *Paradise Regained* together.

CONCLUSION

We can now see that when the seventeenth-century reader first opened his copy of *Paradise Regained* in 1671, he did not find himself upon wholly unfamiliar ground. By far the greater part of the poem would have seemed to him entirely conventional: the presentation of Christ as a human being; the motives ascribed to God and Satan; the disguise assumed by the devil; the use of combat-images; the treatment of the wild beasts; the identification of the wilderness; the ministry of the angels; the *quadraginta dies*; the temptation of bread; and a good deal of the temptation of the kingdoms. Even when the poet felt obliged to break with the tradition, he continued to utilize as much of it as possible, and did his utmost to make sure that his alterations did not violate the best of received opinion. His most startling novelty—the conception of the *mitte te deorsum* —is built directly on elements already inherent in contemporary theology, and is defensible because the interplay of the Matthew-Luke equations made possible the transference of the essential temptation of vainglorious presumption to the *regna omnia mundi*. The introduction of the banqueting scene was equally justified because it presented exactly and unequivocally a temptation already associated with the tradition, but only in either a loose or an unsatisfactory form. The storm scene merely brought into the circle of temptations another which it was frequently admitted that the devil undertook, even though at a later date. The double equation successfully united all these new developments into a basic pattern which did not seriously violate the spirit of the old one. Perhaps the seventeenth-century reader may have suspected that some of the departures from orthodoxy would have been unnecessary if *Paradise Regained* had been written as a tract instead of as a poem. But if he were a liberal and fair-minded critic (and Milton would not have concerned himself over any other), he would have been constrained to admit that every one of the poet's alterations was feasible, and at the best even improved on the conventional view of the temptation by clarifying its

121

ambiguities and bringing out all its latent possibilities to the full.

The modern reader can understand much of Milton's work without referring to the tradition at all. The disguise the devil assumes, for instance, or the motives which led him to undertake the temptation, are clearly presented in the poem itself, and need no other source of information to make them comprehensible. But even so, it is certainly of some interest to set Milton's treatment of a subject against that of the tradition, to see what he rejects and why, to appreciate instances of discrimination and subtlety we could hardly recognize if we did not know the material he began with. And when we turn to topics like the triple equation or the presentation of Christ as a human being, the tradition becomes not an advantage, but a necessity. Unfortunately, as we anticipated at the beginning, Milton often does not trouble to define his terms or to explain himself at length: he takes it very much for granted that everyone of any intelligence will understand the key phrases, the casual allusions, and the implied connections between events that were so obvious and so significant in his own day. And since the more important the hypothesis, the more familiar and hence the less in need of elucidation, the modern reader only too frequently remains deprived of the very facts which it is most essential that he should know, nor is he even so much as conscious of that deprivation. A knowledge of the tradition, of course, will not automatically provide the solution to every problem raised by *Paradise Regained*: since Milton himself left so much to be reconstructed, the answers to many questions must remain in part conjectural, and frankly matters for debate and discussion. Nor would even a full comprehension of what he was trying to do resolve the issue whether it was worth doing at all, or constituted a successful presentation of the subject on the emotional or the poetic level. But *something* can be accomplished. A knowledge of the tradition at least prevents the modern reader from trying to judge Milton's handling of his theme according to the tenets of twentieth-century theology, his memories of what he learned in Sunday School, or his own reading of the Gospels. It keeps him from regarding as heretical and personal much that the seventeenth-century reader would have found conventional and unoriginal.

It indicates the lines which further inquiry and argument may most properly follow. It provides the only sound foundation for an impartial and satisfactory judgment of the work as a whole. He should certainly, therefore, as Milton said in another connection, "be easily inclinable, if he have nothing else that may rouse up his studies, to finish his circuit in an English Concordance and a topic folio, the gatherings and savings of a sober graduateship, a Harmony and a Catena, treading the constant round of certain common doctrinal heads, attended with their uses, motives, marks and means, . . . not to reckon up the infinite helps of interliniaries, breviaries, synopses, and other loitering gear."

BIBLIOGRAPHY

Note: The first item listed is the general reference work, in two series, subsequently referred to as *Patrologiae Latinae* and *Patrologiae Graecae*, the loci for a large number of the individual authors named, whose specified works are there published in entirety.

Migne, J. P., ed. Patrologiae cursus completus; seu, Bibliotheca universalis, integra, uniformis, commoda, oeconomica, omnium S. S. patrum, doctorum scriptorumque ecclesiasticorum, sive latinorum, sive graecorum, qui ab aevo apostolico ad tempora Innocenti III, (anno 1216) pro latinis et ad Concilii florentini tempora (anno 1439) pro graecis floruerunt . . . Series graecae, Paris. 1857-1903 . . . Series latinae, Paris. 1844-1903.

Abingdon Bible commentary. Ed. Frederick Carl Eiselen, Edwin Lewis, and David G. Downey. New York and Nashville. 1929.

Aelfric. Homilies. Reprinted in The homilies of the Anglo-Saxon church. Ed. Benjamin Thorpe. 2 vols. London. 1884.

Allen, Robert. The doctrine of the gospel. London. 1606.

Alulfus. Expositio in quatuor evangelia. Patrologiae Latinae, 79.

Anon. Milton's Latin Bible. Homiletic review 72 (1916). 285.

Anon. The spirit of Cluny. Review of Werner Weisbach's " Religiose Reform und Mittelalterliche Kunst." TLS April 6, 1946, pp. 157-58.

St. Ambrose (Ambrosius). De fide. Patrologiae Latinae, 16.

———. De elia et jejunio. Patrologiae Latinae, 14.

———. Epistolarum classis I. Patrologiae Latinae, 16.

———. Expositionis in Lucam. Patrologiae Latinae, 15.

Andrewes, Lancelot. Seven sermons on the wonderful combat, for God's glory and man's salvation, between Christ and Satan [1592]. Reprinted in Ninety-six sermons. Ed. John Parkinson. Oxford. 1841-43.

Aquinas, St. Thomas. Compendium theologicae (part 1, tractate 2). Trans., Ross J. Dunn. Toronto. 1934.

———. Summa theologica. Ed. Nicolai, Sylvii, Billuart, and C.-J. Drioux. No place. 1868.

Aretius, Benedict. Commentarii in evangelium secundum Lucam. Lansanne. 1596.

———. Commentarii in evangelium secundum Marcum. Lansanne. 1579.

Arias Montanus, B. Novum Testamentum graecum cum vulgata interpretatione. No place. 1584.

Arnobius Junior. Annotationes ad quaedum evangeliorum loca. Patrologiae Latinae, 53.

" Assembly's Annotations." Annotations upon all the books of the Old and New Testament: this second edition so enlarged, as they make an entire commentary on the sacred Scripture . . . by the labour of certain learned divines [1645]. 2 vols. London. 1651.

St. Augustine. Sermon 123. Patrologiae Latinae, 38.

———. Sermo 258. Patrologiae Latinae, 38.

Avanicinus, Nicolas. Vita et doctrina Jesu Christi, ex quatuor evangelistis collecta. Coloniae Agrippinae. 1678.

Baldwin, E. C. " Shook the Arsenal ": a note on *Paradise Regained.* PQ 18 (1940). 218-22.

Bale, J. Brefe comedy or enterlude concernynge the temptacyon of our Lorde and

Saver, Jesus Christ, by Sathan in the desert [1538]. Ed. A. B. Grosart. Fuller worthies library. 1870.

————. The temptation of our Lord [1538]. Tudor facsimile texts. London. 1909.

Banks, T. H. The banquet scene in *Paradise Regained*. PMLA 55 (1940). 773-6.

Barnes, C. L. Error in *Paradise Regained*. NQ 156 (1928). 440.

Barradas, Sébastien. Commentaria in concordiam et historiam evangelicam. 4 vols. in 2. Antverpiae. 1617-22.

Baxter, Richard. A paraphrase on the New Testament, with notes, doctrinal and practical [1685]. London. 1810.

Baxter, W. E. Milton's Bibles. NQ 3 (1911). 109 ff.

Bede. In Lucae evangelium expositio. Patrologiae Latinae, 92.

————. In Marci evangelium expositio. Patrologiae Latinae, 92.

————. In Matthaei evangelium expositio. Patrologiae Latinae, 92.

Bernard, Richard. Rhemes against Rome, or, the removing of the gagg of the new gospell, and rightly placing it in the mouthes of the Romists, by the Rhemists. London. 1626.

————. Thesaurus Biblicus seu promptuarum sacrum. London. 1644.

Beza, Theodore. Annotationes in Novum Testamentum [1564]. Cambridge. 1642.

A new Biblia pauperum, being thirty-eight woodcuts illustrating the life, parables, and miracles of Christ [1470]. London. 1885.

Bilson, Thomas. The survey of Christs sufferings for mans redemption. London. 1604.

Blackwood, Christopher. Expositions and sermons upon the ten first chapters of the Gospel of Jesus Christ, according to Matthew. London. 1659.

Blickling homilies of the tenth century. From the Marquis of Lothian's unique ms. A. D. 971. Ed. R. Morris. Early English Text Society. London. 1880.

Bock, Elfried. Geschichte der graphischen Kunst. Berlin. 1930.

St. Bonaventura, supposed author [Pseudo-Bonaventura]. Meditations on the life of Christ. Trans., Sister Mary Emmanuel. St. Louis. 1934.

Brodribb, C. W. A neglected correction in Milton's *Paradise Regained*, IV, 157-8. TLS, May 17, 1941, pp. 239-41.

Brooke, Stopford. Milton. London. 1879.

Browning, John. Concerning publike-prayer, and the fasts of the church. London. 1636.

St. Bruno Astensius. Commentaria in Lucam. Patrologiae Latinae, 165.

Bucer, Martin. Enarrationum in evangelia Matthaei, Marci, & Lucae, libri duo. Argentorati. 1527.

Bullinger, Henry. Fiftie godlie and learned sermons. Translated from the Latin by H. I. London. 1582.

Bundy, Murray W. Eve's dream and the temptation in *Paradise Lost*. Research studies of the State College of Washington 10 (1942). 273-91.

Caedmon, supposed author. Christ and Satan. Ed. Merrel Dare Chubb. Yale Studies in English 70 (1925).

The Caedmon poems. Trans., Charles W. Kennedy. London. 1916.

Calovius, Abraham. Biblia novi testamenti illustrata. Francofurti ad Moenum. 1676.

Calvin, John. Commentary on a harmony of the evangelists. Ed. and trans., William Pringle. 3 vols. Edinburgh. 1846.

————. Commentarii in quatuor euangelistas . . . quorum tres priores in formam harmoniae sunt digesti: quarto vero seorsim explicatur. . . . Amstelodami. 1667.

————. A harmonie upon the three evangelistes Matthewe, Marke, and Luke, with the Commentarie of M. John Calvine: faithfully translated out of Latine into English by E. P. London. 1610.

————. The institution of the Christian religion. Translated into English . . . by Thomas Norton. London. 1611.

Cajetanus (Thomas de Vio). In S. Marcum commentaria [1530]. Scripturae sacrae cursus completus, 22. Ed. J. P. Migne. Paris. 1862.

Capel, Richard. Tentations: their nature, danger, cure. London. 1636.

Cassiodorus. Expositio in Psalterium. Patrologiae Latinae, 70.

Camerarius, J. Commentarii in novum foedus. Cambridge. 1642.

Cartwright, Thomas. A confutation of the Rhemists translation, glosses, and annotations on the New Testament. No place. 1618.

Chemnitius, Martinus (Martin Chemnitz). Libri tres harmoniae evangelicae. Francofurti ad Moenum. 1600.

The Chester plays. Ed. Hermann Deimling. Early English Text Society. London. 1892.

Chrysostom, St. John. Homiliae in Matthaeum. Patrologiae Graecae, 57.

Chrysostom, St. John, supposed author [Pseudo-Chrysostom]. Sermon on Matthew 4:6-8. Patrologiae Graecae, 61.

Clarke, Samuel. The marrow of ecclesiastical history. London. 1675.

Clericus, Johannes. Harmonia evangelica cui subjuncta est historia Jesu Christi [1699]. London. 1700.

Coccejus, Johannes. Opera omnia theologica, didactica, polemica, philologica. 8 vols. Amstelodami. 1675.

Cordier, Balthasar. Symbolarum in Matthaeum tomus prior [-alter] exhibens catenam graecorum Patrum unius et viginti. Tolosae. 1646-47.

Cory, H. E. Spenser, the school of the Fletchers, and Milton. University of California Publications. Berkeley. 1912.

Cradock, Samuel. The harmony of the four Evangelists [1667]. London. 1670.

Cranmer, Thomas, supposed author. A short instruction into Christian religion being a catechism set forth by Archbishop Cranmer in MDXLVIII: together with the same in Latin, translated from the German by Justus Jonas in MDXXXIX. Ed. Edward Burton. Oxford. 1829.

Crosnier, Augustin. Iconographie chretienne. Tours. 1871.

Daube, David. Three notes on Paradise Regained. RES 19 (1943). 205-12.

Detzel, Heinrich. Christliche Iconographie. Breisgau. 1894.

Didron, A. N. Iconographie chretienne. Paris. 1843.

————. Christian iconography. Trans., E. J. Millington. Completed by Margaret Stokes. 2 vols. London. 1886.

Diodate, John. Pious and learned annotations upon the Holy Bible . . . the third edition, corrected and much augmented. London. 1651.

Dowden, E. Paradise Regained. In: Milton memorial lectures. Oxford. 1909.

Downame, John. The Christian warfare. The third edition, corrected and enlarged. London. 1612.

Du Moulin, Pierre. Heraclitus or meditations upon the vanity and misery of humane life. Trans., R. S. Gentleman. Oxford. 1609.

"Dutch Annotations." The Dutch annotations upon the whole Bible . . . as ordered by the Synod of Dort, 1618 and published by authority, 1637. Now faithfully communicated to the use of Great Britain, in English. Trans., Theodore Haak. 2 vols. London. 1637.

Dyke, Daniel. Two treatises. The one of repentance, the other of Christ's temptations. The sixt impression. London, 1635.

Eliot, John. A harmony of the Gospels. Boston, 1678.

Erasmus, Desiderius. Novum instrumentum . . . cum annotationes. Basel. 1516.

————. In Novum Testamentum . . . annotationes. Basel. 1522.

Erich, O. A. Die Darstellung des Teufels. Berlin. 1931.

Estella, Diegode. Concionatoris in evangelium secundum Lucam enarrationum . . . nunc tandem ab infinitis erroribus, ad sanctae Inquisitionis Hispaniae decreta prorsus elimatus, et summa fide repurgatus. Antuerpiae. 1622.

Fasting. Cyclopedia of biblical, theological, and ecclesiastical literature. 3. 490-4.

Fink, Z. S. The social implications of *Paradise Regained.* JEGP 40 (1941). 482-8.

Fletcher, Giles and Phineas. Poetical works. Ed. F. S. Boas. 2 vols. Cambridge. 1908.

Fulke, William. The text of the New Testament of Iesus Christ, with annotations, by the Papists of the traiterous seminarie at Rhemes. Whereunto is added the translation commonly used in the Church of England, with a confutation of all such arguments, glosses, and annotations. The second edition, revised and enlarged. London. 1601.

Fuller, Thomas. A comment on the eleven first verses of the fourth chapter of S. Matthew's Gospel, concerning Christ's temptations delivered in xii sermons. London. 1652.

Gibbons, Nicholas. Questions and disputations concerning the holy scripture. London. 1601.

Gilbert, A. H. The temptation in *Paradise Regained.* JEGP 15 (1916). 599-611.

Gilhofer, H. and Ranschburg, H., *firm, booksellers, Lucerne.* An important collection of fine and rare engravings and woodcuts by the old masters of the xvth to xviith century. Catalogue no. X. No place, no date [192—?].

St. Gregory the Great (Gregorius Magnus). XL homiliarum in evangelia. Patrologiae Latinae, 76.

Grotius, Hugo. Opera omnia theologica. 4 vols. Basileae. 1732.

H., I. The life of our lord and saviour Jesus Christ. Third edition. No place. 1634.

Hall, Joseph. A plaine and familiar explication (by way of paraphrase) of all the hard texts of the whole divine scripture of the Old and New Testament. London. 1633.

Hammond, Henry. A paraphrase and annotations upon all the books of the New Testament. Third edition, corrected and enlarged. London. 1671.

Hanford, J. H. The temptation motive in Milton. SP 15 (1918). 176-94.

Hartwell, K. E. Lactantius and Milton. Cambridge. 1929.

Heard, Gerald. A dialogue in the desert. New York. 1942.

Heinsius, Daniel. Sacrarum exercitationum ad Novum Testamentum libri xx. Second edition. Cambridge. 1640.

Henniker-Heaton, Raymond. The temptation of Christ by Tiziano Vecelli called Titian. New York. 1925.

St. Hilary (Hilarius). Commentarius in Matthaeum. Patrologiae Latinae, 9.

————. Tractatus in CXXXVIII psalmum. Patrologiae Latinae, 9.

Hildersam, Arthur. The doctrine of fasting, and prayer, and humiliation for sinne. Delivered in sundry sermons . . . in the yeare 1625. London. 1636.

Hunnius, Egidius. De persona Christi. Francofurti ad Moenum. 1585.

Jansen, Cornelius. In Lucam commentaria [1639]. Scripturae sacrae cursus completus, 22. Ed. J. P. Migne. Paris. 1862.

St. Jerome (Hieronymus). Commentarius in evangelium Matthaei. Patrologiae Latinae, 26.

St. Jerome (Hieronymus), supposed author [Pseudo-Jerome]. Expositio quatuor evangeliorum. Patrologiae Latinae, 30.

Junius, Franciscus. Sacrorum parallelorum libri tres: id est, Comparatio locorum scripturae sacrae, qui ex Testamento Vetere in Novo adducuntur. Second edition. London. 1588.

The Junius manuscript. Ed. George Philip Krapp. New York. 1931.

Knox, John. A notable and comfortable exposition of M. John Knoxes, upon the fourth of Matthew, concerning the tentations of Christ. London. 1583. Reprinted in The works of John Knox. Ed. David Laing. 6 vols. Edinburgh. 1856.

Lapide, Cornelius à (1567-1637). Commentarii in IV. evangelia. Antuerpiae. 1712.*

Leigh, Edward. Annotations upon all the New Testament philological and theologicall. London. 1650.

Levron, Jacques. Le diable dans l'art. Paris. 1935.

Lewis, C. S. A preface to Paradise Lost. London. 1943.

Lightfoot, John. A harmony of the gospels [1654]. Reprinted in Works. Ed. John Rogers Pitman. 13 vols. London. 1822-25.

Luca, Francis (Franciscus Lucas Brugensis). In Lucam commentaria [1606]. Scripturae sacrae cursus completus, 22. Ed. J. P. Migne. Paris. 1862.

Ludus Coventriae, or the play called Corpus Christie. Ed. K. S. Block. Early English Text Society. London. 1922.

St. Leo the Great (Leo Magnus). Sermones. Patrologiae Latinae, 54.

Ludolphus of Saxony (le Chartreux). Vie de Jesus-Christ, composée au XVe siecle d'apres Ludolphe le Chartreux; texte rapproche du français moderne par A. LeCoy de La Marche. Paris. 1870.

Luther, Martin. Werke. Ed. J. F. K. Knaake, G. Kawerau, E. Thiele, and others. Weimar, 1883—.

Maldonatus, Joannes. In quatuor evangelistas commentarii. Moguntiae, 1622-24.

Male, Emile. L'art religieux de la fin du Moyen Age. Paris. 1908.

———. L'art religieux après le Concile de Trente. Paris. 1932.

Manton, Thomas. Christs temptation and transfiguration practically explained and improved. London. 1685.

Marlorate, Augustine. A catholike and ecclesiastical exposition of the holy gospel after S. Mathewe. Translated from the Latin by Thomas Tymme. London. 1570.

Masson, D. The life of John Milton. 7 vols. London. 1859-94.

Maurus, Rabanus. Commentariorum in Genesim libri quatuor. Patrologiae Latinae, 107.

———. Commentariorum in Matthaeum libri octo. Patrologiae Latinae, 107.

Mayer, John. A commentarie upon the Newe Testament. . . . the first volume upon the foure evangelists and the Acts of the Apostles. London. 1631.

Menzies, W. Milton: the last poems. Essays and studies by members of the English Association 24 (1939). 80-113.

Miller, R. D. Milton's conception of the temptation as portrayed in Paradise Regained. MLN 15 (1900). 202-5.

Milton, John. Paradise regained. Ed. E. H. Blakeney. London. 1932.

———. Paradise regained, minor poems, and Samson agonistes. Ed. M. Y. Hughes. New York. 1938.

———. Paradise regained, with notes of various authors. Ed. Thomas Newton. London. 1785.

———. Complete works. Ed. F. A. Patterson [the Columbia edition]. 18 vols in 21. New York. 1931-38.

More, Henry. The life and doctrine of our saviour Jesus Christ. Gant. 1656.

Musculus, Wolfgangus. In evangelium Matthaeum commentarii. Basel. 1544.

Natale, G. Evangelicae historiae imagines ex ordine evangeliorum quae toto anno in missae sacrificio recitantur. No place. 1593.

Origen. In Lucam homiliae. Patrologiae Graecae, 13.

* Not published in his life time.

————. Scholia in Lucam. Patrologiae Graecae, 17.

Pareus, David. In S. Matthaei evangelium commentarius. Oxford. 1631.

Pattison, Mark. Milton. New York. 1880.

Perkins, William. Satans sophistrie answered by our saviour Christ, and in divers sermons further manifested. London. 1604.

Phillipps, E. M. The frescoes in the Sixtine chapel. London. 1901.

Piscator, Johann. Analysis logica libri S. Lucae. London. 1597.

————. Analysis logica evangelii secundum Matthaeum. London. 1594.

Poole, Matthew. Annotationes upon the Holy Bible [1680]. Edinburgh. 1801.

Price, John. Commentarii in various Novi Testimenti libros. London and Oxford. 1660.

Radbertus, St. Paschasius. Expositio in Matthaeum. Patrologiae Latinae, 120.

Ravenellus, Petrus. Bibliotheca sacra, seu thesaurus scripturae canonicae amplissimus. Geneva. 1650.

Rupertus Abbas. In quatuor evangelistarum commentariorum liber unus. Patrologiae Latinae, 167.

Raleigh, W. Milton. London. 1914.

Rice, W. G. Paradise regained. Papers of the Michigan Academy of Sciences, Arts, and Letters 22. 493-503.

Roberts, Francis. Clavis Bibliorum: the key of the Bible. London. 1675.

Ross, Alexander. Virgilii evangelisantis Christiados libri xiii. Rotterdam. 1653.

Saurat, Denis. Milton: man and thinker. New York. 1925.

Scultetus, Bartholemaeus. Diarium humanitatis domini nostri Jesu Christi in terris. Franckfurt an der Oder. 1600.

Speculum humanae salvationis [Coleridge-Boxall-Richee ms.]. Ed. M. R. James. Oxford. 1926.

Stannihurst, Wilhelm. Dei immortalis in corpore mortali patientis historia moralis doctrinae placitis & commentationibus illustrata auctore. Editio secunda correctior. Antuerpiae. 1664.

A Stanzaic life of Christ, compiled from Higden's Polychronicon and the Legenda aurea (Harley ms. 3909). Ed. F. A. Foster. Early English Text Society. London. 1926.

Taylor, Jeremy. The great exemplar of sanctity and holy life . . . described in the history of the life and death of the ever blessed Jesus Christ . . . with considerations and discourses. London. 1657.

Taylor, Thomas. An exposition of Christ's temptations. No place. 1618.

Theophylactus. Enarratio in evangelium Lucae. Patrologiae Graecae, 123.

————. Enarratio in evangelium Marci. Patrologiae Graecae, 123.

————. Enarratio in evangelium Matthaei. Patrologiae Graecae, 123.

Tillyard, E. M. W. Milton. London. 1934.

Trapp, John. A commentary or exposition upon all the books of the New Testament. Second edition, " very much enlarged throughout." London. 1656.

Twelfth century homilies in ms. Bodley 343. Ed. A. O. Balfour. Early English Text Society. London. 1909.

Udall, John. The combate betweene Christ, and the Deuill. Foure sermons on the temptations of Christ. London. 1589.

Valla, Laurentius. Annotations in Novum Testamentum. Basilae. 1540.

Velmatius, Johannes Maria. Veteris et Novi Testamenti opus singulare. Venice. 1538.

Vertue, Henry. Christ and the church: or parallels, in three books. London. 1659.

Vida, Marcus Hieronymus. The Christiad. Translated into English verse by Edward Granan. London. 1771.

Walafridus Strabus. Expositio in quatuor evangelia. Patrologiae Latinae, 114.

————. Homiliae in Lucae. Patrologiae Latinae, 114.

————. Glossa ordinaria. Patrologiae Latinae, 114.

Ward, Richard. Theologicall questions, dogmaticall observations, and evangicall essays, upon the gospel of Jesus Christ, according to St. Matthew. London. 1640.

Welles, John. The soules progresse to the celestiall Canaan. London. 1639.

Whatley, William. Prototypes, or, the primarie precedent presidents out of the book of Genesis. Shewing, the good and bad things they did, and had, practically applied to our information and reformation. London. 1640.

Wild, Johann. In sacro sanctum Iesu Christi domini nostri evangelium secundum Matthaeum. Paris. 1564.

[Woodhead, Abraham]. An historical narration of the life and death of our Lord Jesus Christ. Oxford. 1685.

Wyclif, John. Select English works. Ed. T. Arnold. 4 vols. Oxford. 1869.

Xavier, P. Hieronymus. Historia Christi Persice conscriptus . . . Latine reddita & animadversionibus notata a Ludovico de Dieu. Lugduni Batavorum, ex officina Elseviriana. 1639.

York plays; the plays performed by the crafts or mysteries of York, on the day of Corpus Christi in the 14th, 15th, and 16th centuries [Ashburnham ms.]. Ed. L. T. Smith. Oxford. 1885.

Zigabenus, Euthymius. Commentarius in quatuor evangelia. Patrologiae Graecae, 129.

INDEX

PLATES

The following plates are taken from the extra-illustrated Kitto Bible (Vol. 34, L. 1886) in the Huntington Library, San Marino. California. They are reproduced by permission of the library. The number in parenthesis on each refers to the page in the Bible where it may be found.

PLATE I (6351 [upper])

Of JESUS being Baptized, and going into the Wildernefs to be Tempted.

The Baptifme of Iefus

S. MAT. 3. 17.

And lo, a voice from heaven, saying
This is my beloved Son, in whom I am
well pleafed

The Temqtation of Iefus

S. MAT. 4. 10

Get thee behind me Satan For it is
written Thou shalt worship the Lord
thy God and him only shalt thou ſarue

PLATE II (6361 [verso-upper])

CVM PRIVILEGIIS.

Plate III (6350)

Accedens tentator dixit ei, si filius Dei es, dic vt lapides isti panes fiant. Matt. 4.

PLATE IV (6358 [lower])

Hat die der Satan dü in schweeren Nahrungß Zeiten ·
Dü solt auff Gottes macht deß wagen in gefahr ·
Will Er durch geld Ehr Pracht dich blenden ü' verleiten ·

Stell dich mit Gottes wort grüßet dapffer dar-
Erwegend daß man mir allein Gott soll anbeten
Und dienen · wie hier dü die Engel auch herbetten

Epist. 2. Cor 6 v. 10

Laß Gottes Gnade nicht an dir vergeblich werden
Bedenck die gnaden Zeit · um wahr den tag des Heyls ·
Ihr hirten sonderlich der theur vertrauten heerden

Gebt ja kein Aergerniß und anstoß eures theils
Daß niemand Euer Amt mit Lastern könn beschmeissen
Als Gottes diener Euch stets trachtet zu erweissen

24

PLATE VI (6352 [lower])

Plate VII (6360)

JEsus wird vom Teufel versucht.

Jésus est tenté du Diable.

MATTH. IV. MARC I. & LUC IV.

PLATE VIII (6362 [upper])

19

Tentator Christo monstraverat omnia Regna,
     quicquid et eximii magnus hic orbis habet.
Ast is perfrictæ frontis verbo increpat hostem,
     ausum supremi carpere jura Dei.
It præceps Satanas summo de vertice montis:
     assistit Iesu turba ministra polo.

Der Teuffel schenket zwar so vil Er nur kan zeigen,
damit der Herr sich soll anbetend vor Ihm beugen.
     Kriegt aber eins aufs Maul, und ziehet die Pfeiffen ein,
     Anhörend das man Gott anbetten soll allein
Du unverschamter Geist magst wol von hinnen weichen,
die Engel kommen an pack dich zu deines gleichen.

PLATE IX (6357 [lower])